Praise for _Ask_
(al *as How to Interview*

By Paul McLaughlin

"This is the best book I know about an activity that has become central to our culture."
— **Robert MacNeil, former co-host,**
The MacNeil/Lehrer Report

"This humane, intelligent, insightful book is not only useful but also a very good, entertaining read."
— **Patrick Watson,** *chair, CBC*

"It is a gold mine of lore and method invaluable for anyone who Monday morning has to go out and earn their living talking to strangers."
— *The Toronto Star*

"If you like interesting people and reading about them—as well as if you are a person who interviews or is interviewed—*Asking Questions* is the book for you."
— *The Vancouver Province*

"To Paul McLaughlin, interviewing is a delicate and complex skill that, at its best, demands constant practice, constant improvement, and constant reappraisal."
— *The Ottawa Citizen*

"In *Asking Questions*, McLaughlin includes 10 interviews that are models of their kind."
— *The Kingston Whig-Standard*

"This thoughtful and exhaustive book has a lot to tell novices and experienced writers about how to get total strangers to trust you long enough to really say something."

— **Caitlin Kelly,** *The Montreal Gazette*

"We just don't listen well, says McLaughlin. The more deeply we listen, the more eloquently people will speak."

— *The Edmonton Journal*

"This book is packed with useful information."

— *Canadian Author & Bookman*

"*Asking Questions* will probably be snapped up by journalism departments as required reading, but it's entertaining for the rest of us."

— *Canadian Business*

"He probes every interview imaginable—from the daily scrum outside the Parliament Buildings in Ottawa, to the one-on-one in-depth talks on television news shows and business magazines."

— *The Guelph Mercury*

"Good practical knowledge for any person involved in interviewing. Moreover, the book [is] really funny in parts."

— *Canadian Public Administration*

"When it comes to interviewing, who among us cannot admit to room for improvement. This book will help us all explore that room. To read *Asking Questions* is to explore, enjoy and to benefit."

— **Barrie Zwicker, publisher,** *Sources*

"A neat little book [that] examines the media interview from every imaginable angle."

— **Ross McLean,** *Broadcast Week*

"Effective interviewing—it's an art."

— *The Oakville Beaver*

"The strength of the book is the authority derived from more than 100 interviews in the research phase."

— *Content: Canada's National News Magazine*

ASKING THE BEST QUESTIONS

A comprehensive interviewing handbook for journalists, podcasters, bloggers, vloggers, influencers, and anyone who asks questions under pressure.

By Paul McLaughlin

Author of *Asking Questions: The Art of the Media Interview*

Centennial College Press

Copyright © Paul McLaughlin, 2022
Library and Archives Canada Cataloguing in Publication

Title: Asking the best questions: a comprehensive interviewing handbook for
    journalists, podcasters, bloggers, vloggers, influencers, and anyone who asks
    questions under pressure / by Paul McLaughlin.
Names: McLaughlin, Paul, 1950- author.
Description: Includes bibliographical references and index.
Identifiers: Canadiana (print) 2022028539X | Canadiana (ebook) 20220285446 |
Subjects: LCSH: Interviewing in journalism. | LCSH: Interviewing in mass media. |
    LCSH: Interviewing—Technique. | LCSH: Interviews.
Classification: LCC PN4784.I6 M36 2022 | DDC 070.4/3—dc23

ISBN 9780919852853 (softcover)

Centennial College Press
951 Carlaw Avenue
Toronto, Ontario
M4K 3M2

Editor: Jeremy Lucyk
Intern: Isabel Federgreen
Design: Reilly Ballantyne

Printed and bound in Canada.

Visit us at:
centennialcollegepress.ca
paulmclaughlin.ca

To my children, Arianna and Roone

CONTENTS

Chapter One: The preamble 21
   The Trump effect 22
   The war of interviewing 23
   Sidebar: Interviewing alert 24
   Not a manual 24
   Sidebar: Gender-neutral language 25
   My background 25
   Sidebar: Some of my best friends 27

Chapter Two: Educate yourself 28
   Work on general knowledge and vocabulary 29
   Sidebar: Advice from a Hall-of-Famer 32

Chapter Three: Be genuine .33
   You don't have to act tough 34
   Sidebar: Emulate Oprah 36
   Compassion 36

Chapter Four: Understand the other side 38
   The microphone as a death ray 39
   It could damage my reputation or career 41
   What if I say something stupid? 43
   Scientists and other professionals 43
   Sidebar: Oprah, how did I do? 46
   Possible disconnects 46
   Sidebar: Don't look me in the eye 47

Chapter Five: Accept the role. 48
Sidebar: How to interrupt 49
Sidebar: Like paddling a canoe 50

Chapter Six: Getting the interview. 51
Don't just email. 53
Writing an interview request 54
Using a third party. 55
Media and communication departments 58

Chapter Seven: Location, location, location. 60
The power of location 60
The medicine cabinet ruse 62
Be imaginative. 64
Sidebar: The walking interview 64
Background woes 64

Chapter Eight: What do I have the right to ask? 67
The key word is "relevant" 69

Chapter Nine: Preparation. .71
*Sidebar: What color socks did you wear on
your first heist?* 72
Bone up. 73
Preparing questions 75
The cost of not knowing 76

Chapter Ten: What are you walking into? 80
Sidebar: Four Basic Types of Guests 81
Wrong assumptions. 82
Not as prickly as advertised. 83
Sidebar: Who is the interviewee talking to? 84

Chapter Eleven: Role-playing and visualization......86

Like chess 88

Confrontational and emotionally charged interviews. 91

Don't be bullied into attacking 92

Chapter Twelve: Be conversational 95

A *pas de deux* 96

We all make mistakes 97

Chapter Thirteen: It's okay to be shy 99

What if I'm young and have a high voice?........ 101

Chapter Fourteen: Asking a person's age...........102

Chapter Fifteen: We're not the police 105

Give them a reason 106

Ambush interviews 107

Going undercover and hidden cameras 109

Chapter Sixteen: Transitioning to performance mode .112

**Chapter Seventeen: Invasive personal questions
and sexism** 115

*Sidebar: Should male journalists be allowed to
  interview female celebrities in glossy magazines?* 118

Alarm bells should go off. 119

Flirting. 121

Sidebar: Interviewing transgender guests 122

Sidebar: Mean tweets....................... 123

Chapter Eighteen: Interviewee demands 124

This often works 125

I want to see the article or hear the broadcast
 beforehand 125
What do you say when asked to share a draft? 127
When might you share? 127
*Sidebar: An expert on whether journalists should
 let sources look over stories before publication.* . 130

Chapter Nineteen: When difficult conditions
 are imposed 132
 Off the record 134
 The post-comment condition 136

Chapter Twenty: Comfort the afflicted/afflict
 the comfortable 139
 Hold their feet to the fire 140
 We don't do PR 142
 Sidebar: Walter Cronkite's liberal take 142
 Sidebar: Noam Chomsky on being embedded 143
 Objectivity 143
 Sidebar: It doesn't have to be sweet, Caroline 144

Chapter Twenty-one: Brain-based interviewing 145

Chapter Twenty-two: Trust and rapport 150
 Trust 151
 Rapport 152

Chapter Twenty-three: Listening 156
 Listen up 156
 A skill to work on 157
 Sidebar: Avoid distractions. 158
 Our job is to reveal 159

Sidebar: We all miss something 160
Sidebar: What to listen for 160
Why we don't listen 161
You easily can miss things 162
Sidebar: Listen to Hemingway 163

Chapter Twenty-four: Silence 164
How silence helps an interviewer 166
Allow time to recall 168
Sidebar: The director's cue 169

Chapter Twenty-five: Tone 170
Why should interviewers care about tone? 171
No one likes the sound of their own voice 173
Sidebar: Tone and meaning must match 173
Sidebar: A killer confesses 174

Chapter Twenty-six: One question at a time 176

Chapter Twenty-seven: Open and closed questions . . . 178

Chapter Twenty-eight: Following up on answers 180
Sidebar: Keep asking 181

**Chapter Twenty-nine: Coming up with
the next question** 182

Chapter Thirty: D&A, the lifeblood of features 184
Details 184
Specifics 185
Anecdotes 186
Sidebar: Look for connections 189

Chapter Thirty-one: Slow down 191
  Interviewing elderly people 193
  The speed of stress. 194

**Chapter Thirty-two: Don't answer
your own questions** 196
  The right way to do it 199

Chapter Thirty-three: Interviewee fatigue 201
  Sidebar: Poetic injustice 204
  What if you have to ask tired, old questions? 205

Chapter Thirty-four: The broadcast interview. 207
  Some foundation required 209
  Sidebar: David Frost on the interview subtext 210
  The need for a dynamic 210
  The audience 212
  Sidebar: Be totally present 214
  Sidebar: Off-camera interviews 214

Chapter Thirty-five: The print interview 216
  Recording the interview. 217
  Sidebar: Zoom interviews 218
  Lasting longer 219
  Sidebar: When writing or recording isn't possible . 221
  Sidebar: What they have a right to know 222

Chapter Thirty-six: Telephone and email interviews . .224
  Don't dial too soon 226
  Sidebar: The voice can say a lot 227
  The email interview. 228

Chapter Thirty-seven: Streeters 230

Chapter Thirty-eight: Difficult interviews 232

    Quiet resolve 234

    Dealing with appalling viewpoints. 236

    Find a way in. 238

    If the interview becomes problematic. 239

    Sidebar: Necklace and heels 241

    Sidebar: One-Minute Answers 242

Chapter Thirty-nine: Don't apologize for a question . .244

Chapter Forty: What if they question me? 245

Chapter Forty-one: Interviewing victims 248

    Respect the victims 250

    Sidebar: Terminology 251

    After the interview. 252

    Resources to help. 252

    Sidebar: Many want to talk 255

    Sidebar: A call for empathy 256

Chapter Forty-two: Interviewing minors 257

    Sidebar: Fear not the children 260

    Sidebar: The CJR's advice 260

Chapter Forty-three: Long preambles 262

Chapter Forty-four: Avoid "utmost" questions 266

Chapter Forty-five: Bad verbal habits 268

    How do you feel about this question? 269

    Sidebar: A better feel for the question 272

Chapter Forty-six: Some people say. 273

Chapter Forty-seven: Reading body language 276

What if you're wrong? 279

Sidebar: Women's intuition 281

Our own body language 283

Chapter Forty-eight: Manage the interview 284

Before the interview. 285

What if you're attacked prior to an interview? 288

During the interview 289

Chapter Forty-nine: The most important question . . .292

Chapter Fifty: The final question 294

Acknowledgements 297

References 299

Index 321

Subject Index. 321

Name Index. 324

About the Author. 329

For the purpose of this book, the terms "print" and "broadcast" define the two primary types of interviews. Print refers to any interview that doesn't have an audiovisual component; and broadcast to any that, in whole or in part, is seen or heard on TV, radio, or online.

I recognize that some print interviews include recorded clips, but they are principally conducted for the written word.

ONE: **THE PREAMBLE**

My first book on this subject, *Asking Questions: The Art of the Media Interview*, was published in 1986, before the Internet and social media dramatically changed our lives.

This new book also focuses on journalism interviews, but it's also written for podcasters, bloggers, vloggers, influencers, HR professionals, and investigators. It will be useful for anyone who poses questions as part of their livelihood or creative pursuits.

To put the new markets into perspective, podcasthosting.org estimates that as of June 2021 there were two million podcasts worldwide; growthbadger.com puts the number of blogs at 600 million. Many of the creators on these innovative platforms need to conduct interviews to develop some, or most, of their content.

The journalistic-style interview, therefore, is no longer the exclusive domain of people working in traditional media. On the contrary, they could now be the minority.

The vast majority of the advice I present in this book is practical. But interviewing can include some psychological and philosophical aspects, as well. After all, we're talking to people under pressure, sometimes a considerable amount. How we respond to these circumstances can vary, depending on each person (both the interviewer and the interviewee).

I offer my insights on these aspects with the full understanding that I could be wrong, or that my take on what happens when people communicate might not be in accord with yours. That's understandable. The only thing that really matters, I believe, is that we do our work with an awareness of how difficult it can often be to both ask and answer questions.

If that's your underlying approach, you should be well on your way to conducting successful interviews.

THE TRUMP EFFECT

The overwhelming majority of the literally thousands of interviews I've conducted over the years have been polite, enjoyable, and conflict-free.

But not all. Some have been confrontational, unpleasant, antagonistic, awkward, frustrating, or a combination of some or all of those elements.

However, the interaction between journalists and interviewees today is more fraught with suspicion and mistrust than ever before, largely due to former U.S. President Donald Trump. His all-out assault on the media—"fake news," "enemy of the people," and "lamestream media"—undermined one of the pillars of democracy: freedom of the press.

I'm not going to explore the reasons why Trump waged war on the fourth estate, an attack many of his supporters cheered. But I do need to say that he has poisoned the media landscape; all of us who ask questions for a living need to understand that it has had, and continues to have, an impact on what we do. Trump tainted the well of public trust in journalism, perhaps forever.

Interviews that are essential to journalistic investigations or that demand accountability—with politicians, for example—have always been combative to some degree. And celebrities might object to questions they think are too probing or intrusive.

Now, thanks to the Trump era, those who are so inclined can throw the "fake news" blanket over us as they refuse to answer or engage in a line of questioning that makes them uncomfortable.

Consequently, interviewers need to know how to deal with difficult or uncooperative people more than ever before.

THE WAR OF INTERVIEWING

I'm a great admirer of Steven Pressfield's wonderful book on creativity, *The War of Art*. As Pressfield emphasizes, when it comes to realizing our artistic ambitions, the real war is with ourselves. He calls our self-imposed constraints "resistance," by which he means the barriers we put up that keep us from achieving our creative goals.

I believe the same happens with some interviewers. Our resistance can manifest in several ways, such as: not conducting sufficient research; not bothering to prepare an interview plan; having our phones or tape recorders do the listening; not committing to a line of questioning; and, especially, being afraid to ask a challenging question.

In my interview training sessions, I always ask: do you think it's predominantly the guest who won't answer a difficult question or is it, more commonly, that the interviewer is afraid to ask it? By far, participants say it's the latter.

Few of us have been taught the skills required to, among other tasks, pose a question that could very well upset the other person—perhaps even generate an angry, hostile, or threatening response. Consequently, some interviewers shy away from asking certain critical questions; or they ask them in an inappropriate tone, which can close up the interviewee.

I hope *Asking the Best Questions* provides some guidance to help overcome the fears and levels of resistance that I believe most, if not all, interviewers experience to some degree.

INTERVIEWING ALERT

Professionals need to be extremely alert, at an almost preternatural level. Whether the interview is friendly, hostile, or somewhere in between, the interviewer must be willing and able to commit to the process in a way that's not common to most human interactions. How often are we only partially "there" during a conversation with a family member, friend, or someone we just met? How often do we stop listening or zone out?

But that can't be the standard for a media interview. Being there—being completely there—is one of the fundamentals of successful interviewing.

NOT A MANUAL

This is not an interviewing manual. No book or article can tell you exactly what to do during an interview. Rather, *Asking the Best Questions* is my subjective take on what might transpire when talking to people—usually strangers—when there's something at stake. Some of what lies ahead might resonate with you; some might not.

I encourage you to employ and experiment with the advice you think makes sense and disregard any techniques that make you uncomfortable, or with which you disagree.

A key to interviewing is to develop your own style, one that fits your personality, ethics, and interpretation of how an interview works or should work.

The one thing I stress, though, is that whatever style you adopt, and whatever techniques you rely on, have them come from a place of clarity and thoughtfulness. Make conscious decisions, not reactive ones (although this will inevitably happen at times), about what you're asking and why.

I consider interviewing, when done properly, an art. I believe all interviewers have an obligation to study it as best they can.

GENDER-NEUTRAL LANGUAGE

Throughout the book, the pronoun "they" will be used to represent an individual in a gender-neutral fashion. Similarly, I'll use "them," "their," "they're," and "themselves" to avoid the awkward "he/she," "him/her," etc.

MY BACKGROUND

My approach to interviewing has evolved from three interconnected segments of my professional life: journalism, teaching, and corporate and government communications.

The first interview of my career was in 1973, when I worked as a researcher for a daily CBC Radio program. Since then, I've done countless others as a chase producer, news reporter, on-air interviewer (radio and TV), magazine and corporate writer, and author.

For more than four decades, I've taught journalism students: at Algonquin College and Carleton University in Ottawa; and at the Ryerson (now Toronto Metropolitan University) School of Journalism and York University (in its professional writing program) in Toronto. Teaching has heightened my awareness of the challenges and fears many face as they begin their careers.

In the 2000s, I also served as the principal interviewing trainer for CBC Radio and TV journalists and hosts. Some were starting out; others had been in the business for decades.

Freelance corporate and government communications work exposed me to the media interview from the other side, providing invaluable insights about what it's like to be on the receiving end of a journalist's questions. In this capacity, I've coached former senior law enforcement officers (who switched to private practice), investigative accountants, and senior government bureaucrats, among others, on how to handle themselves in an interview.

The foundation of this book emanates from these three strands to feed one overriding interest: what happens when an interviewer and an interviewee talk to each other.

Lastly, I want to emphasize that those we interview are not clips or quotes or sound bites. They are real people and deserve to be treated as such. I think it's a privilege to talk to a variety of new people on a regular basis. Some are amazing and inspiring, some have clay feet, and some are downright nasty. It's fascinating to learn from them all and, perhaps, in the process, discover new things about ourselves too.

SOME OF MY BEST FRIENDS

I personally know quite a few of the people quoted in this book. Rather than revealing my relationship each time, which could become annoying, I'm using this overall disclaimer. However, occasionally I'll mention a connection, if I think it's required.

KEY TAKEAWAYS

- Develop your own interviewing style; there is no manual that tells you exactly what to do in a particular situation.
- It's more often that an interviewer is afraid to ask a difficult question than an interviewee doesn't want to answer it.
- Most interviews you conduct will be friendly and enjoyable; you have to know how to deal with the small number that aren't.

TWO: **EDUCATE YOURSELF**

TV interviewer Larry King famously bragged that he never did research.

On December 31, 1999, the eve of the new millennium, he proved how foolhardy that could be. His guest was the Dalai Lama, one of the most important and best-known spiritual leaders in the world. "Your Holiness, is this a new millennium for you in the Muslim year?" King began. "Do you celebrate this as a year for your holy day?"

Evidently, King believed the Dalai Lama was a Muslim, a member of a faith that was celebrating the year 1420, based on the Hijri or Islamic calendar, in 2000.

The Dalai Lama graciously mentioned his Buddhist faith in his answer, to help the hapless King from further embarrassing himself. But the intransigent interviewer was not done insulting the holy man. At the end of the interview (a brief snippet is available on YouTube), King concluded by thanking him for "sharing this time with us and whatever year it is in your faith or whatever. Happy New Year to you."

That level of ignorance is unforgivable. I have no idea how King processed his gaffe, but I know that if I had made such a colossal mistake, I would carry the memory (and the shame of it) with me the rest of my life.

I sense that *Today* show presenter Kathie Lee Gifford would be similarly burdened by what happened during an interview with actor Martin Short in May 2012. Short was on a promotional tour for his movie *Madagascar 3: Europe's Most Wanted* when she steered the conversation towards his personal life, specifically his long and much-celebrated marriage to fellow Canadian actor Nancy Dolman.

"[You] and Nancy have one of the greatest marriages of anybody in show business," Gifford said. "How many years now for you guys?"

"Thirty-six years," Short responded.

"But you're still, like, in love?" Gifford said.

Short forced a small smile. "Madly in love. Madly."

What the actor didn't say was that his wife had died of ovarian cancer two years earlier.

Most people would have not been as kind as Short. And they might have asked, or at least wondered, how a national TV host could have decided to extol his marriage without having done even a shred of research to make sure they were still together, never mind that she was still alive.

WORK ON GENERAL KNOWLEDGE AND VOCABULARY

I doubt there's a journalist who has not experienced a cringeworthy moment during an interview, either by saying the wrong thing or by displaying ignorance of something they should have known. I certainly have.

Most interviewees assume journalists are aware of what's happening in the world, have an above-average knowledge of history, geography, and politics, and possess a decent, if not exceptional, vocabulary.

That's why I give my journalism students pop quizzes about people and current events. The results are often depressing. Few could name prominent world leaders, identify the dates of major world events (one said World War I ended in "the mid-1990s"), or answer basic citizenship questions (a third-year student said Canada's population was approximately 1.5 billion).

When I test them on assigned readings (to inspire them to read the articles), it's evident that few looked up words whose definitions they didn't know, even though they could have done so easily on their phone. I still get a word-a-day sent to my computer; almost none of my students subscribe to this free service.

But they're not stupid. Quite the opposite. They're very smart and quick-thinking, but fact-weak (many, but not all). The generation raised with the Internet, and with information available instantly on a phone, has perhaps become accustomed to finding information by looking it up whenever they needed to access it. (Mind you, pre-Internet students also struggled with my tests.)

It's helpful to have a mobile "library" but, as I say in my classes: "You can't look up a person's biography or a historical date during an interview."

Try to learn something new every day. If you read a prominent person's name and don't know who it is, or come across a helpful fact that's unfamiliar, stop and look it up.

Take the citizenship test for your country. Can you pass it?

Know the location of the major countries in the world and their leaders. Can you find, say, Belgium on a map? Or Madagascar?

Research key events over the last century or so (such as wars, economic depressions, major weather events). Act as if you're preparing to be a contestant on *Jeopardy*.

Last and most important: read as much as you can. During a guest lecture, a student once asked David Hayes, one of Canada's top feature writers and writing teachers, for his most important advice to writers. His answer applies equally to interviewers.

"READ, READ, READ," he wrote on a blackboard in large, capital letters. "Every successful writer, of fiction or nonfiction, reads widely and deeply. Anything that is text on the page is something to potentially learn from, but obviously, seeking out the best nonfiction and fiction you can find will be the best models for your own writing." To which I would add, WATCH and LISTEN to examples of good and poor interviews.

If you're not reading, keeping up with the news, and deconstructing interviews, but want to work in journalism, that's a disconnect. It would be like finding a musician who never listens to music, or a film director who never screens movies.

I once asked the accomplished author John Irving (*The World According to Garp*, et al.) why he was so much more successful than many other writers. "I work harder," was his immediate reply.

Preparation, intention, and effort: these are the not-so-secret secrets to success.

ADVICE FROM A HALL-OF-FAMER

When reporter Shi Davidi of Sportsnet, the Canadian national sports specialty service, first started covering the Toronto Blue Jays, one of the game's top writers shared an insight. It was Bob Elliott, the Toronto Sun *baseball reporter who was later inducted into the National Baseball Hall of Fame and Museum.*

"After 20 years covering baseball, I understand how little I know about the game," Elliott said. "We all think we know a lot about sports, but we really don't. Maybe we get 15 to 20 percent of what goes on behind the scenes."

KEY TAKEAWAYS

- Educate yourself, in all ways possible, as part of your interviewing training and development.
- Know as much as you can about those you intend to interview.
- Study successful and unsuccessful interviews.

THREE: **BE GENUINE**

In a poignant opinion piece for *The New York Times*, published in late November 2020, Meghan Markle, the Duchess of Sussex, wrote about the searing pain of having gone through a miscarriage about four months earlier.

In her frank op-ed, she also referenced an interview she'd had with ITV's Tom Bradby, a friend of her husband Prince Harry. It took place in October 2019, as she and Harry were ending a long tour in South Africa.

"I was exhausted. I was breastfeeding our infant son, and I was trying to keep a brave face in the very public eye. 'Are you OK?' [Bradby] asked me. I answered him honestly, not knowing that what I said would resonate with so many—new moms and older ones, and anyone who had, in their own way, been silently suffering.

"My off-the-cuff reply seemed to give people permission to speak their truth. But it wasn't responding honestly that helped me most, it was the question itself. 'Thank you for asking,' I said. 'Not many people have asked if I'm OK.'"

What Bradby did that day in 2019 was talk to Markle as one human being to another. He obviously had some kind of relationship with her through his friendship with her husband, but I'm going to assume he would have acted the same way no matter what.

I think some journalists, for a variety of reasons, forget their human side during an interview, especially if it might involve difficult or challenging questions. Perhaps it's a fear that if they show their soft side at the outset, they won't be able to ask tough questions later. I don't have that concern. I'm comfortable talking to a guest the way I would a friend or colleague, no matter what may lie ahead.

YOU DON'T HAVE TO ACT TOUGH

Aspiring journalists sometimes struggle with how to behave on the job.

They don't want to be seen as soft or a pushover, so they overcompensate and act tough. They imagine that success in the profession requires them to be extremely aggressive, unethical, even obnoxious. Hardboiled eggs, I call them.

Some imitate journalists who behave unethically in movies or TV. One example is the depiction of Kathy Scruggs in the 2019 biopic *Richard Jewell*, directed by Hollywood legend Clint Eastwood. A real-life reporter with *The Atlanta Journal-Constitution*, Scruggs broke the story that identified Jewell—the security guard who discovered a bomb at Atlanta's Centennial Olympic Park during the 1996 Summer Olympics—as the FBI's prime suspect.

The story ultimately proved to be false, but not before it destroyed Jewell's life. (He died in 2007, at age 44, after receiving financial settlements from several media outlets.)

In the movie, Scruggs (who died in 2001 of a morphine overdose) was depicted as trading sex for stories, a claim that infuriated many who knew her, including those at her newspaper. While some movies lionize reporters, such as 2015's *Spotlight*—in which journalists at *The Boston Globe* investigated accusations of systemic child abuse by Roman Catholic priests—it's common for reporters to be seen as hard-drinking cynics willing to bend, if not break, the rules to get a story. Sticking a microphone in someone's face, recording their words and how they look, and scribbling down (not always accurately) what they say in response to questions (not all asked nicely), can be an awkward interaction for both parties, especially if they're strangers. I've never (thank God) had to be part of a pack chasing a person down the street while yelling out questions or accusations. That approach almost never elicits anything of value beyond some predictable visuals and, to me, contributes to a negative impression of the media.

Now, don't get me wrong: I'm a great believer in the greater good approach. If by stealing a document a reporter uncovers, say, an environmental disaster, then by all means steal it. But as we asked students at Carleton University's School of Journalism when I taught there, "Is it okay to lie and cheat and steal to prove that someone lies and cheats and steals?"

EMULATE OPRAH

Oprah once said: "When I was 19 years old, I interviewed [the Reverend] Jesse Jackson as a young reporter in Nashville. And he said to me then, 'One of your gifts is being able to be yourself on TV.'

"So, when I moved to Chicago, and I was up against the then 'King of Talk' [Phil Donahue], my boss at the time called me into his office and said, 'Listen, we know you'll never be able to beat him. So just go on the air and be yourself.' So, I have made a career out of my own authenticity. I feel that I have made a living being myself."

COMPASSION

I believe journalists should be compassionate, even towards those we don't like or agree with. That doesn't mean we condone what they do.

"My approach (when reporting) is that could be my town, that could be my house, my loved one at the center of that story, and how would I want them to be treated at that moment?" says Lester Holt, the anchor for *NBC Nightly News*. "In my opinion, there is a lot of room for compassion in what we do."

Our role is to reveal rather than to judge, to inform rather than condemn. As the character Ted Lasso advised in an episode of his eponymous program, misquoting the poet Walt Whitman: "Be curious, not judgmental."

What can be gained by telling a murderer you find murder reprehensible? It's more than likely going to close the person down than shed light on why someone takes another person's life.

That doesn't mean you have to pretend to be fine with what the interviewee did. You can be yourself without having to put on a false front.

Imagine this exchange instead:

Q: What was it like to kill the person?

A: I enjoyed it. It was exciting. You should try it.

Q: I'm certain it wouldn't excite me. However, why do you think it did that for you?

As the Dalai Lama so wisely puts it: "If you want others to be happy, practice compassion. If *you* want to be happy, practice compassion."

KEY TAKEAWAYS

- Be genuine.
- Be curious.
- Don't be judgmental.

FOUR: **UNDERSTAND THE OTHER SIDE**

While working on *Asking Questions*, a friend, an award-winning magazine writer, agreed to be interviewed for the book. He was known for his exceptional reporting and fluid writing style.

For about 20 minutes, I probed the tricks and techniques he used to gain people's trust, so they would open up to him. Suddenly, he stood up, left my living room, and ran out into the street. "I can't do this," he said, visibly upset. He was referring to the experience of being interviewed. He found it too uncomfortable to be asked to "justify" (his word) what he did for a living. Nothing I said could convince him otherwise. The interview was over.

As I mulled over what had happened, I hoped my friend had learned something of considerable value: that some people find the process of being interviewed incredibly stressful. I think all but a few interviewees experience a degree of discomfort, ranging from a little to a lot.

Most interviewers don't like it when the tables are turned. I can attest to that from the distrust I often encountered during the years I wrote about the media for *TV Guide*, and from some of the negative replies I received when I requested interviews for *Asking Questions*.

One of the industry's giants, the hardnosed interrogator Mike Wallace, was a famously shy interviewee. "As an interview subject himself, Mike Wallace is guarded," journalist Harry Stein wrote in a 1979 article about *60 Minutes* for *The New York Times*. "During one recent session, he snapped off the reporter's tape recorder every time the conversation edged into what he deemed sensitive territory." Imagine a politician doing that to Wallace.

I believe it's extremely beneficial for interviewers to get a taste of what it's like to be interviewed; in fact, I think it's an experience we should seek out. As Atticus Finch said in *To Kill A Mockingbird*, "You never really understand a person until you consider things from his point of view, until you climb inside of his skin and walk around in it."

THE MICROPHONE AS A DEATH RAY

Actress Tallulah Bankhead, who performed in more than 300 film, stage, TV, and radio productions, talked about the fear that would overcome her when she had to, as one example, be interviewed on live radio. "As I faced the microphone, it assumed the guise of a contraption that might let loose a death ray," she said. "I had a feeling such as I experienced when an ether cone was slipped over my nose. There was a pounding in my ears, a buzzing in my head. My hands grew frosty. A dank dew coated my brow. My first word sounded like the caw of a crow."

In 2010, model Kate Moss told *The New York Times Style Magazine* that she hated doing interviews. "When I first started, I did press because I wasn't really aware that they would write something really negative, but then they did, and I was like, 'Oh no, I don't want to go back there. I don't really want to open myself up to that kind of criticism.'"

Some people dislike dealing with the media for philosophical reasons.

Howard Dean, former Democratic governor of Vermont and a 2004 presidential candidate, reflected on his views about the profession in *Politico Magazine,* in 2015. "The press is still free and is still able to bring up issues that nobody else is willing to bring up," he said. "In their core role, they still do what they have to do. But in terms of educating the public, their credibility has gone way down. The press is one of the failed institutions in American democracy, along with Wall Street and Congress.

"Today, I think it's much more gotcha questions, much less substance, much more interest in the gossipy—and more getting it first, not getting it right. The inside-the-Beltway press is just the worst. There's too much reliance on unnamed sources, which are unreliable and can't be evaluated by the reader. And the willingness to engage in pack journalism is just appalling."

Noam Chomsky, whom *The New York Times* called "the top intellectual alive" and "one of the most quoted scholars in history," is rarely seen on network U.S. TV. Why? He's too radical for an institution that, primarily, endorses the status quo; as well, he refuses to reduce the complexity of his thoughts into sound bites.

"The mass media," he says, "serve as a system for communicating messages and symbols to the general populace. It is their function to amuse, entertain, and inform, and to inculcate individuals with the values, beliefs, and codes of behavior that will integrate them into the institutional structures of the larger society. Any dictator would admire the uniformity and obedience of the U.S. media."

I can't imagine interviewing Chomsky without having read some of his seminal works. (I suggest *Manufacturing Consent*, which was also made into a documentary.) I wouldn't talk to Howard Dean about politics without studying his campaign for the presidency, during which one brief moment in a speech was seen as a death knell on the road to the White House. (Watch "The Scream That Doomed Howard Dean" on YouTube and decide for yourself whether his unbridled yell during a rally justified the scorn and armchair psychoanalysis that ensued.)

It's important, therefore, to be alert to the potential that an interviewee might be guarded due to prior experiences. If your research reveals their animosity or suspicion of the process, it might be wise to talk about their concerns, and your understanding of the media's role, before starting an interview.

IT COULD DAMAGE MY REPUTATION OR CAREER

Some are concerned about what could go wrong during an interview. Do they have a reason to worry? Can one interview derail a career or reputation?

You bet it can. Just ask Prince Andrew.

In 2019, he agreed to an hour-long interview with BBC presenter Emily Maitlis about his relationship with convicted pedophile Jeffrey Epstein, who had committed suicide in prison a few months before. Instead of ending speculation about his involvement in what appeared to be a child sex ring, Prince Andrew fueled it.

As *PR Week* noted, "PR professionals have been left gobsmacked by the tactics and execution of Prince Andrew's BBC interview…labelling it one of the worst PR disasters of all time." Five days after the interview aired, the Queen announced her son would "step back from public duties."

There are numerous other examples of interviews that came back to bite the interviewee, sometimes incredibly hard.

It happened to David Ahenakew, former National Chief of the Assembly of First Nations and member of the Order of Canada. Following a speech in 2002, during which he made disparaging remarks about immigrants and Jews, a reporter for the Saskatoon *Star Phoenix* asked Ahenakew to clarify what he'd said. He reiterated what he had said, was subsequently charged with a hate crime, and had his prestigious Order of Canada rescinded.

The prominent First Nations figure ultimately was acquitted of the hate-crime charge. He claimed, among other reasons for his comments (caught on tape), that he is diabetic, and on the day of his speech his blood sugar was out of control.

I'm in no way suggesting that either of these men (or any others caught doing something apparently wrong) should evoke our sympathy. Rather, I need to point out that these and countless other examples abound in the public psyche. Consequently, they can make potential interviewees nervous that they might say the wrong thing. And possibly suffer serious consequences.

WHAT IF I SAY SOMETHING STUPID?

Famous people sometimes say things that are inane or boneheaded. In 1981, actress Brooke Shields told *Omni* magazine that, "Smoking kills. If you're killed, you've lost a very important part of your life." Although she was only age 16 at the time, it's a quote that lives on the Internet to this day.

Pop superstar Justin Bieber likely regrets what he wrote in the guestbook at the Anne Frank House in 2013, when he was almost 20 years old. After touring the home where the young diarist hid from the Nazis for several years during World War II (she died in Auschwitz concentration camp in 1945), he penned: "Truly inspiring to be able to come here. Anne was a great girl. Hopefully she would have been a Belieber," as many of his fans are called. This tone-deaf, self-centered comment likely will follow him to his obituary.

Potential interviewees easily can find examples of ill-advised comments during interviews and may be wary about being added to the idiocy canon.

SCIENTISTS AND OTHER PROFESSIONALS

At the beginning of the 1980s, Environment Canada commissioned me to write a magazine-style booklet that explained the environmental threat of acid rain, in clear and non-scientific language.

It was a high-profile issue at the time. When newly elected President Ronald Reagan visited Ottawa in March 1981, protestors greeted him on Parliament Hill.

Their placards called for an end to acid rain caused by the coal-producing states in the Ohio Valley. (Canadian industry contributed to it, too.)

When I began interviewing the government's experts on acid rain, to obtain quotes for the booklet, I was met with what seemed, to me at least, to be unwarranted resistance. I knew these men and women cared deeply about the problem, so why were they so reluctant to help me? I asked a senior scientist what was going on.

"They don't like you calling it acid rain," he said.

"Why?"

"Because it's not accurate. It's actually wet and dry deposits of acidic precipitation. Not just rain. The acid in the atmosphere can also come down with snow, smog, that kind of thing. They're concerned that if you quote them saying 'acid rain' they'll look uninformed, ignorant, un-scientific."

I hadn't understood these scientists were so concerned about how their peers would react to what they said. They were much less concerned with what I might think of them because I was not their primary audience.

Immediately, I changed my approach. From then on, before each interview, I assured the scientist that my document would define acid rain accurately, then note that it's commonly known as acid rain. If they balked at this concession, I said the following:

"I know you want to reduce and eradicate this problem. Did you see any signs on Parliament Hill saying, 'Stop Wet and Dry Deposits of Acidic Precipitation?' Or did they say, 'Stop Acid Rain?'" The reference to the Reagan demonstrations tended to do the trick.

The lesson? When dealing with professionals who might employ what we consider jargon, it's important to understand their concerns. Many need to feel comfortable with how we'll portray what they say about a technical issue. Journalists tend to be contemptuous of bureaucratic language (although we readily use our own buzz words), but maybe we should be less rigid about this. Maybe there's a way to meet everyone's needs.

There are other contributing factors as to why a person might be reluctant to grant an interview. Kate Moss said this in *NYT Style Magazine*: "I think that a lot of the time you walk in a room [and] they already know what they want to write about you, so it doesn't matter what you're like." Is it possible she's right? Not always, but it does happen.

What can also occur is this: after a few Google searches that say so-and-so is a so-and-so, some journalists set out to confirm the claim, rehashing old issues or old failures.

For years, the UK press called Nick Faldo "El Foldo." For years he reigned as one of the world's greatest golfers and was subsequently knighted, but early in his career he wasn't living up to the media's standards of achievement. Until he began to win big tournaments, he was dogged with questions (by people, most of whom had never come close to winning anything noteworthy) about his missed opportunities. Eventually, he won six major tournaments, including three Masters titles, proving his critics wrong.

How would you react if your past transgressions or failures were constantly brought up, perhaps in a mocking tone? Could that close you down? Make you mistrustful?

If you present yourself as an open person, interested in the past but only raising it because it has a legitimate bearing on the present, interviewees will likely be less defensive towards you. I also think it's the right way to be.

OPRAH, HOW DID I DO?

Oprah Winfrey says there is one question almost all her guests ask her, after the cameras are turned off. She includes former presidents George W. Bush and Barack Obama, and singer Beyoncé, among those who have posed it.

"After every interview, you know what they would say? 'Was that okay? How was that? How did I do?' So I started to say, 'Wow, that's so interesting. Beyoncé is asking me if she was okay, after she just taught me how to twerk.'"

What does this tell us? That no matter how famous and powerful a guest, most people you're interviewing, at heart, just want to do well.

POSSIBLE DISCONNECTS

Before an interview, I quickly ask myself what might cause a disconnect between myself and the guest. They include:

- *Age*: A 25-year-old interviewing a 70-year-old (or vice versa) could encounter language and cultural barriers.
- *Gender*: For example, would a female assault survivor perhaps respond differently to me than to a female interviewer?
- *Culture*: If the interviewee comes from a different ethnic, religious, or cultural background, likely there are factors that should be taken into account. You may need to research the person's culture.

- *Socioeconomic status*: A poorly paid reporter might resent a wealthy executive or athlete.
- *Profession*: If, for example, you believe all chemical companies are evil, that could affect how you approach an interview with an executive from a chemical company about a benign issue.

This is not a definitive list, but the principle is important to consider before conducting an interview. We all have biases and life experiences that color our perceptions of people. As an interviewer, it's critical to think ahead about what they are, and to do one's best to guard against them having a negative effect on the outcome of an interview.

DON'T LOOK ME IN THE EYE

If you've been raised to believe a truthful person looks you in the eye, research whether this "rule" applies to all cultures.

In some Asian cultures, for example, it's considered disrespectful to maintain eye contact with others. The degree of eye contact can also be affected by a person's profession or social position.

KEY TAKEAWAYS

- Being interviewed can be stressful for interviewees.
- Some professionals, such as scientists, are worried their comments might be misunderstood or trivialized by an interviewer.
- Truthfully assess whether you have any biases that could negatively affect how you conduct an interview.

FIVE: **ACCEPT THE ROLE**

This is a brief but vital message: If you decide to interview someone, you must accept the role of being the interviewer, no matter how nervous or insecure you might feel.

Too often, I've seen interviewers engage in an interview without really understanding their role and responsibilities.

As the questioner, you have a certain amount of power as long as you don't relinquish it out of fear or from a lack of awareness.

In theory, interviewers steer the conversation in a certain direction, although it can often veer from that path. You ask the questions and explore or challenge the answers, while avoiding having to answer any questions thrown back at you (with some exceptions).

It's the interviewer's responsibility to interrupt a long-winded or evasive answer, to keep track of how much time has passed, and whether enough time remains to accomplish all the set goals of the interview.

Some interviewees will try to take control of an interview. If that happens, it's your responsibility to stop the subject from hijacking the conversation. This could require you to interrupt and shift the conversation back in the direction you believe to be the right one.

Almost all sophisticated interviewees are media trained. They're taught to "bridge" a question they don't want to answer in order to change the subject. If this happens, you have to be alert and in control, returning to the question you need answered, perhaps by re-bridging: "I'm sure that's an interesting point you just brought up, but I still want to ask you about…" or words to that effect.

Accepting the role also requires a commitment to what you hope to accomplish during the interview. A clever person might try to move you away from a line of questioning they don't want to deal with. They may try intimidation: "You can't ask me that;" "That's too personal;" "Don't be ridiculous;"; or, as Donald Trump said to a CNN reporter when he was president, "What a stupid question. I watch you a lot and you ask a lot of stupid questions."

Sometimes, they will attempt to convince you to focus on another area: "What I think you really should be asking is X" or "Let me tell you a great story about X." (A caveat: ask yourself if they're actually offering good advice. Some interviewees bridge to a meaningful or more pertinent point.)

Overall, you need to believe in your focus, and fight for it. As Vince Lombardi Jr. once said, "Most people fail not because of a lack of desire but because of a lack of commitment."

HOW TO INTERRUPT

You need to interrupt a guest who is going on too long or wandering off topic.

I suggest this three-pronged approach: interrupt, acknowledge, bridge:

- *Actually interrupt, using hand gestures to reinforce the interjection, if the interview is in-person.*
- *Say something such as, "I'm sorry to interrupt," then acknowledge that the person's answer has been helpful before redirecting the conversation. "What you just told me was really helpful, but now I'd like to…"*
- *Bridge to the next question, perhaps offering a reason for the interruption. "But there's so much I want to ask you in the time we have together, so now I'd like to…"*

LIKE PADDLING A CANOE

"Think of an interview as a canoe," says Vicki Kreuger of the Poynter Institute. "The source should do all the hard work—the paddling—of answering the questions. As the interviewer, you should do the steering. Different kinds of questions can guide the conversation in different ways."

KEY TAKEAWAYS

- Accept and study the role of the interviewer.
- Know how to interrupt.
- Commit to the questions you believe should be answered.

SIX: **GETTING THE INTERVIEW**

The most creative way I obtained an interview involved Bob Rae. In 1990, he was elected the first (and to this point the only) New Democratic Party premier in Ontario's history. Not long into his first term, *Cottage Life* magazine commissioned me to interview him about his cottage memories. I assumed he'd enjoy the chance to discuss something non-political.

As always, my first step was to contact his media office. If time permits, it's important to follow the proper protocol.

I remember, as a rookie researcher for CBC Radio (I'd never gone to journalism school, so I learned by trial and error), phoning Buckingham Palace and asking if it was possible to talk to the Queen. She was soon to visit Ottawa and some kerfuffle had arisen at City Hall about her trip. An impeccably polite man informed me that Her Majesty was not available at the moment, but he could take her a message. I imagine it was immediately dispatched to the nearest rubbish bin, as the Brits call it.

If you want to interview someone "important," for want of a better word, ask yourself whether they have staff responsible for arranging interviews. It's not always obvious. If they work for a company or organization that has a media or communications division listed on their website, that's a logical place to begin.

Many entities have an in-house policy that requires employees to funnel all interview requests through the media office. That's certainly the case for government bureaucrats. Cabinet ministers and other high-ranking politicians also use media or communication professionals to handle requests. Opposition members are usually more willing to take calls from journalists directly.

Senior corporate executives also tend to depend on their PR departments. But not always. I've contacted some CEOs directly and they've been happy to discuss a possible interview. If not, they'll ask you to call their media office.

Many are extremely hard workers, so I've occasionally phoned early in the morning and caught them at their desk. Andrew Crosbie, one of Newfoundland's most successful businessmen, agreed to an interview when I called his direct office line at 7:00 a.m. his time.

Bob Rae's media office was not helpful. I contacted it several times and left messages explaining what I was proposing, but no one responded. A woman I finally got through to made it clear she considered *Cottage Life* to be of little, if any, interest to the premier.

I pointed out the magazine's considerable readership (most of whom lived in Ontario), their demographics (cottages can be more expensive than many urban homes), and its array of national magazine awards. "Send me a letter," she said, "and try to convince me." She didn't sound convincible.

Several weeks after mailing such a letter, I received a polite reply from the premier's office thanking me for my job application but informing me that all positions had been filled. The writer wished me well in my future job searches. Needless to say, this annoyed me.

With an imminent deadline, I decided to take a more direct approach. A friend gave me Rae's home address. I couriered him a letter outlining my attempts to arrange an interview, ending with the job-application insult. I also included what I hoped was a funny Top Ten list of reasons he should agree to talk to me. (They were popular at the time because of *The Late Show with David Letterman*.)

The next day, an extremely cold-voiced staffer phoned to arrange a call with the premier. He and I had a great talk, and I wrote a well-received article.

I don't recommend intruding on a prominent person's home territory unless all other attempts have failed (or there's breaking news that requires an immediate reaction). In this case, I felt justified in dealing with the premier directly. Obviously, he agreed.

DON'T JUST EMAIL

A young writer with a university newspaper sent me an email in late 2020 requesting an interview about a campus issue. Unfortunately, it went into my spam folder. By the time I found it, the deadline had passed.

At no time did the person follow up with me: by phone, through social media, or by sending another email. This lack of initiative is by no means the case with all young journalists, but I have often witnessed it with my students—and also with some experienced journalists.

In progress reports they submit while working on their magazine articles, it's apparent some of my students sent an email to a prospective interviewee and then waited, sometimes for more than a month, for a response.

When I suggest they should have also phoned or used social media to contact the person, many express concern that this would be coming on too strong, or a form of harassment.

It's not, as long as all the messages are polite and professional. If, when you get in contact with the person, they mention, perhaps with surprise and sometimes annoyance, the numerous ways you employed to reach them, explain that you have a deadline and must use all possible avenues of communication. Almost everyone, upon hearing this, understands.

WRITING AN INTERVIEW REQUEST

It's normal to first request an interview by email. The subject line is critical. I typically use, "Media Interview Request." But any such wording will do, as long as the purpose of the message is clear.

Opening your message with, "My name is…" marks you as a rookie. Tell the person right away why you're writing. Clearly and concisely explain the story you're working on, where it will be published or broadcast, and add a few words about yourself (if applicable). The message should be polite, professional, and without grammar, punctuation, or spelling mistakes.

You must proofread it before pressing "send." Get into the habit of doing this.

Your job is to chase/pursue, which means that if you don't get a response by a certain date (and how long you wait will depend on your deadline), send another email. (You can always say you were concerned your first one went to spam, which does happen.) If you have their number, phone the person and/or post a message on social media.

You're not intruding or invading a person's privacy. You're simply doing your job, hopefully in a courteous manner. The recipient can agree or decline.

Finding people is another essential part of your job. The Internet, of course, is where most of us start. If you can't find a person's email on Google or another search engine, see if the place where they work has an email template. For example, it may be first name, period, last name, @companyname. Try that for the person you want to contact.

If nothing online helps, telephone the company/organization and explain to the receptionist that you need to send the person a media interview request and ask for the person's contact information. They often comply.

USING A THIRD PARTY

It's often beneficial to consult someone who knows an elusive target interviewee personally. Ask them to suggest a strategy to reach or convince the person to be interviewed. It likely will be helpful to say the mutual contact suggested you call, as if you share a common friend.

That's what two CBC Radio broadcasters in Ottawa did when they were collaborating on a documentary on Muhammad Ali. Bob McKeown and Robert Harris found "The Greatest" was as elusive to pin down for an interview as he was to catch in the ring.

They followed him from New York to New Orleans, Miami, and Las Vegas, never able to penetrate the phalanx of guards and hangers-on who crowded around him. With their deadline looming, they had all but given up. Their only hope was a man named Harold Conrad, who had befriended them, and was a member of Ali's most trusted inner circle.

A former boxing reporter for the *Brooklyn Eagle* and the promoter of one of Ali's first fights, Conrad was revered by Ali because he supported Ali when the boxer was stripped of his title after refusing to be drafted for the Vietnam War.

Conrad gave them Ali's unlisted number in Chicago and prescribed the following: "Tell him I told you to call. Call him The Champ. He likes to be called The Champ. Tell him you're from the Canadian government. He likes governments."

At a suggested time, McKeown phoned and a refined female voice answered, "The Ali residence."

"Hello. Bob McKeown from the Canadian *Government* Broadcasting Corporation calling. Harold Conrad arranged for me to call The Champ. Is The Champ there?"

About 30 seconds later, there was a barely audible grunt from the other end of the line. "Hello, Champ?" Another grunt. "Champ, I'm from the Canadian *Government* Broadcasting Corporation. Harold Conrad arranged for me to call. We're preparing a documentary on you, and we'd like to come and do an interview."

There was about a minute of abject silence. "Uh...how much you getting for this? How much are you paying me? If you talk to my lawyers and agents, they know how much I'm worth."

"Listen, Champ. If you knew how little we're getting

for this you'd be utterly embarrassed," McKeown replied honestly. That seemed to disarm the mumbling voice. "We can't afford to pay you anything, because we're not making anything ourselves. It's a labor of love."

With that declaration, Ali's tone changed abruptly. The interview was arranged for the next day. And he gave McKeown and Harris directions to give the taxi driver at the airport so they wouldn't be overcharged.

When they arrived the next day, Ali had forgotten about the conversation, but welcomed them in. Five hours and a long, rambling interview later, they reluctantly declined an invitation to dinner because they had to fly back to Ottawa for work the next day.

Another way to connect with an elusive person is to approach a journalist who has previously interviewed someone you've not been able to reach.

CBC Radio producer Talin Vartanian used this tactic to line up an interview with Mohamed ElBaradei, a prominent scholar and diplomat, widely viewed at the time as Egypt's president-in-waiting. None of her many efforts through the usual channels had worked, so Vartanian phoned a print journalist at the *Cairo Times* who had interviewed ElBaradei for a profile.

The woman said he had no time for PR people, including his own, but ElBaradei trusted his brother. She gave Vartanian the brother's contact information, and that led to the CBC interview.

During their phone conversation, Vartanian told the reporter that if she ever needed help with a story from Canada, she'd be happy to return the favor. As it turned out, that later happened.

MEDIA AND COMMUNICATION DEPARTMENTS

Any company or organization of a reasonable size has media/communications professionals who help arrange interviews. Not all are cooperative (it depends a lot on the story) but, by far, my experience has been that they do their job well. Many are former journalists, or have gone to journalism school, so they understand what you need and why deadlines matter.

Not enough people take advantage of this resource. Nor do they realize that in some enterprises it's imperative to contact the PR people first. That doesn't mean you have to comply with whatever regimen the company imposes. If need be, and if you feel righteous about it (as I did with Premier Rae), you can bypass this level of compliance. But if you have the time to do it right, why wouldn't you?

If the PR person seems reluctant to help, one response is to mention, truthfully, that the story will be presented with or without their client's involvement. You might say, "We will have to say that we offered you the opportunity to comment but you declined."

It's also important to know that, thanks to the Internet, people have gathered together through websites, chat rooms, and other forums to share their experiences regarding virtually every issue, health problem, desire, cause, or…well, I doubt there's an end to the list.

If you contact someone identified on one of these sites, especially an organizer or moderator, that person will likely be able to help you. If they can't, ask if they know someone who could.

Finding an interviewee can be like detective work. You keep talking to people and following up on information until you get to the right person. And, like any good bloodhound, you don't stop until you've exhausted every possible outcome. That's what a determined journalist does, always.

KEY TAKEAWAYS

- Follow up on interview requests after a reasonable time (if a deadline is looming, that could be within hours).
- Don't just rely on email or social media to contact a potential interviewee; also use the telephone.
- If time permits, first go through the proper channels, such as a communications or media office.

SEVEN: **LOCATION, LOCATION, LOCATION**

Experienced broadcast interviewers, especially those who work on camera, instinctively consider the location of an interview. The backdrop is important to the presentation of their story, and it might affect an interviewee's mood or reaction to questions.

Veteran magazine writers also know it's critical to have "scenes" for their features. You can't produce an engaging profile of several thousand words unless you take the reader with you to locations where the central character, and sometimes minor characters, are involved in interesting or meaningful experiences that advance the story. It only makes sense, and not just for major projects. It can also apply to short broadcast and print pieces.

Interviewees tend to be amenable to a location suggested by a camera crew, probably because they've been conditioned by a lifetime of TV watching; I've found them less likely to agree for a print assignment. It might take a bit of explaining as to why you want a certain location for an assignment with no obvious (to them) visuals.

THE POWER OF LOCATION

If you take a war veteran back to the site of a critical battle, their recollections likely will be far more vivid and emotional than if the interview took place in a coffee shop. If you interview a police officer in the store where they thwarted a robbery and saved the owner's life, the answers likely will be far more powerful and detailed than if it took place at the officer's desk.

When I was writing magazine features, I always wanted access to the main character's home, if possible.

Canadian Business once assigned me to write a cover story about an American entertainment industry executive. He had been parachuted into Toronto to lead a major player that was at war with a rival company. I was told he was granting just this one interview, and I had access to him for only one day.

First, I negotiated the circumstances with his firm's PR director. Initially, she told me I had to come to his office. Our conversation went something like this:

PM: That won't really work for me.

Her: Why not?

PM: I need to see him in action, not sitting behind a desk. Is he doing anything interesting in the next while? Any meetings, speeches, that kind of thing?

Her: He's going to a meeting with a design firm that's presenting him with a new-look concept for our entire chain, in about a week from now. If he agrees to let you come along, would that be okay?

I jumped at the opportunity, and it paid off. I quietly sat at a boardroom table for most of a day, as a major Toronto firm introduced its vision of the company's new image. During the presentation, my profile subject so badmouthed the CEO of his main competitor that, when I quoted him in my first draft, the magazine's lawyers said some of it was defamatory and had to be removed.

At the end of many hours together in a meeting room, the profile subject begged to call it a day, but I didn't want to. I was eager to see where he lived and asked if we could do one last interview later that day in his home, which turned out to be a luxury condo overlooking Toronto's harbor.

One of the main criticisms leveled at him was that he was in Canada for only a short time and would leave once he had done unpleasant corporate actions, such as firing a lot of people. He vehemently protested that wasn't true, that he wanted to plant roots in Toronto, despite his track record of never staying in a new destination for long.

When we got to his condo, I was certain the critics were right. The apartment didn't have a single personal effect other than a framed picture of his son. He admitted, when I delicately pointed this out, that he had a high-end designer come in and stage the place. In no way did his residence suggest this was a man who planned to be there for an extended period of time.

Seeing where he lived emboldened me to lean on the angle that he had been brought in to do some dirty work, then move on to his next cleanup job (which proved true). It not only gave me a scene on which to end my piece but helped me feel confident in presenting that notable allegation.

THE MEDICINE CABINET RUSE

It used to be much easier to gain access to a person's home. The rapscallion magazine writer Earl McRae once described how he exploited the opportunity:

"I always go into someone's medicine cabinet," he said. "I always make a point of excusing myself and going to the can even if I don't have to. Often medicine cabinet doors make a little noise when you open them. So I'll flush the toilet at this point. Medicine cabinets are fascinating. Often, they'll reveal a person's anxieties, ego. You might find Grecian Formula [hair coloring], maybe eye shadow in a bachelor's apartment. Might belong to a girlfriend, who knows? But when you come out you might get the conversation around to ego, vanity, just to see if there's anything there."

Just for the record, I have never snooped through a person's medicine cabinet, nor will I ever, for obvious ethical reasons. But I do look around whatever rooms I'm invited into. I like to examine the décor, whether the place looks lived in, what books are evident (if any), art on the walls, trophies, etc.

I was once conducting an interview in the office of a senior executive who presented himself as a mild-mannered person. I noticed there were no pictures of his family, although I knew he was married and had a child. An absence of family pictures is quite rare in someone's office. But he did have pictures of himself at several international car rallies, which he and his partner hadn't won, but had placed extremely well in.

When I asked about the photographs, his face lit up. He began to describe the rallies in an animated manner, and I immediately saw a very aggressive side to him, not the quiet soul he had presented himself to be. It helped me understand him better.

BE IMAGINATIVE

It's true in this day and age that many interviewees want to keep their business and personal lives separate. They don't want you having access to their private spaces. I understand that.

But too many print interviewers, faced with that response, opt to meet at a Starbucks or a Tim Hortons. At minimum, think of a place that's interesting.

THE WALKING INTERVIEW

Writer Pierre Berton told me he liked to take authors to bookstores.

"I once interviewed Christopher Morley, who was then a very well-known American novelist and on the board of the Book of the Month Club," Berton said.

"He said to me, 'I feel the coefficient of civilization in any given city is in its secondhand bookstores.' And I said, 'Then why don't you and I go around and look.' And the interview was conducted in secondhand stores as we opened books and talked about them. That's what I call the walking interview or the moving interview."

BACKGROUND WOES

For broadcast, be mindful of background sounds that could distract from your interview. If you want an example, search YouTube for an interview conducted by the comics Bob and Ray in New York's Times Square. Bob, in character as inept reporter Wally Ballou, asks

Ray about his cranberry farm, as all hell breaks loose in the background. Despite sirens and gunshots, Ballou continues to question Ray on matters of little consequence or interest, especially compared to what seems to be happening around them.

When I was a radio interviewer one of the first things I would do before starting an interview conducted away from the studio was to listen to the ambient sound in the remote location. If I felt it would distract listeners, I'd insist we find a better environment for the conversation or devise a way to reduce or eliminate the noise.

This can also be an issue for non-broadcast interviews that are taped. Clattering dishes in a restaurant, as one example, can be loud and make it difficult to hear, when transcribing, what the interviewee said.

When interviewing a female, I'm always sensitive to concerns about safety. In the late 1970s, I had a CBC assignment to interview Quebec actress Céline Lomez for a series on the childhoods of famous Canadians. She had recently appeared on the cover of *Maclean's* magazine, on the heels of her role in the 1978 Canadian heist film *The Silent Partner*, along with Elliott Gould and Christopher Plummer. I contacted her directly and we discussed where to meet.

She was a tad apprehensive until I suggested the bar at the Ritz-Carlton hotel in Montreal, a public location where I accurately sensed she would feel safe and in control.

I remember the 25-year-old as warm and forthcoming. She laughed easily when I asked the bartender if he would turn down the music in the bar, as I knew it would make it difficult to hear her on the tape. When he saw who I was interviewing, he readily agreed. Since then, I have found that a hotel lobby or lounge, which is often an interesting backdrop, works well when meeting a female interviewee outside of her workplace.

It's possible you'll have no choice where an in-person interview takes place. The subject's office or a nearby coffee shop seem to be the default choices. You can't force a person to open their home to you or to meet you at a location you think would be best suited to the purpose of the interview.

However, do take time to think of where the conversation(s) could take place. And, as Mahatma Gandhi, Stevie Wonder, and other famous people have said, "If you don't ask, you don't get." The answer just might be yes.

KEY TAKEAWAYS

- Consider what location to suggest for an out-of-studio interview, as it could have a beneficial effect.
- When in an interviewee's office, home, or other location they spend time in, observe the décor, and any books, art, or other personal items.
- Be aware of any ambient sounds that could make it difficult to hear the interviewee when playing back the recording for broadcast or transcribing.

EIGHT: WHAT DO I HAVE THE RIGHT TO ASK?

In May 2007, about five months after Nicolas Sarkozy had been elected president of France, he reluctantly sat down in Paris with *60 Minutes* correspondent Lesley Stahl for an interview. It was prior to an upcoming trip to America, and he made it clear from the outset that he was in no mood for the conversation, calling his press secretary "an imbecile" for having arranged it.

Near the end of the interview, Stahl brought up a topic dominating watercooler conversations in France: rumors that Sarkozy and his wife Cécilia were having marital problems.

"Since we've been here, it seems that every day we're hearing another story about your wife. What's going on?" Stahl asked.

"If I had to say something about Cécilia, I would certainly not do so here," the president replied in French.

"But there's a great mystery. Everybody's asking. Even your press secretary was asked at the briefing today."

"Well, he was quite right to make no comment. And no comment, *merci*," he said. Sarkozy removed his translation earpiece, shook Stahl's hand, patted her on the left shoulder, and said "*bon courage*," meaning "good luck." Then he walked off.

Two weeks later, the Sarkozys announced they were divorcing.

Was Stahl justified in asking about their marriage? Absolutely, in my opinion. He was a world figure whose personal life was not only of interest to the public but might have an influence on how he exercised his duties as president.

Was Sarkozy justified in walking out? He had a right to, but I think it was a mistake. His tantrum did not seem presidential. Better to have sideswiped the question with a quiet, controlled response: "This is a personal matter between me and my wife, as I'm sure you can understand and respect. I will not answer any questions about it." Then stay put.

If he had said something along those lines, I doubt the clip from the interview would still be online. YouTube features countless other examples of interviewees, mostly celebrities, abruptly ending an interview when they're asked something they didn't want to answer.

Some interviewers are uncertain whether they can ask a question they expect might be rebuffed by the interviewee.

They offer reasons such as:

- I don't want to upset the person.
- It's too personal.
- I don't know whether I'm allowed to ask it.
- I don't feel comfortable asking something that's embarrassing or controversial or too emotionally raw.
- The interviewee will get mad at me.
- The interviewee will walk out.
- The interviewee's PR person will be angry and never deal with me again.

I understand these concerns, and some could prove to be accurate; but they should not derail you from asking the right questions. But how do you know if a question is "right?"

THE KEY WORD IS "RELEVANT"

I believe that once a sophisticated interviewee (someone who knows how the media works) has agreed to an interview, the person has entered into an unwritten agreement that gives the interviewer permission to ask any relevant question.

I would never randomly ask interviewees about their sex life or sexual orientation. It's none of my business. But if I had interviewed Ted Haggard, the prominent U.S. evangelist, when news broke about his use of crystal meth with a male prostitute, questions about his sex life and sexuality would have been essential. Not to ask them would have been unprofessional, especially since Haggard publicly denounced homosexuality and drugs from his pulpit.

I don't care what someone does in their bedroom, but if a public figure displays that level of hypocrisy and foments hatred against a group in society for something they, themselves indulge in, that's relevant and it has to be addressed.

What if they walk out? I'm asked that a lot. My answer: wonderful. I would consider it a badge of honor if a reasonable question, asked in a respectful manner, triggered that reaction. Walking out is a very clear answer. Let's hope it's caught on video.

Another pertinent word is "fair." Was it a fair question, one that an average, reasonable person would expect to be answered?

If so, an interviewee who abruptly ends an interview after being asked a fair question has spoken volumes, revealing an unwillingness to even consider a question that a reasonable person would want answered.

You can't be a successful interviewer if you're afraid to ask questions that might upset the guest or their handlers. Focusing on relevance can help you determine whether your questions should be posed, no matter the anticipated response.

KEY TAKEAWAYS

- You have a right to ask a fair and reasonable question, even if it upsets the guest.
- Don't worry about an interviewee walking out. It's often a revealing answer.
- Don't be afraid to ask a challenging question you know has to be asked.

NINE: **PREPARATION**

"If you want to flop as an interviewer, fail to prepare." The prestigious Poynter Institute for Media Studies, a non-profit journalism school and research organization in St. Petersburg, Florida, couldn't have stated it more plainly.

Roy MacGregor, one of Canada's top writers, adds: "Great writing is great research. The further you go into the research, the more you understand what's really going on in a story."

How much research and preparation you conduct will depend on several factors:

- *The time available prior to the interview.* Sometimes, a story is assigned just before the interview has to take place. When that's the case, I ask myself two essential questions on my way to the interview: What's the story about? And what's my first question?

- *How much time has been allotted for the interview.* If you've only been promised a few minutes, or there are only a few questions you need answered, your preparation, obviously, is very focused on whatever angle you're pursuing. Longer interviews, especially those for magazine articles, documentaries, or books, can last up to several hours. The scope of your research for these can be extensive.

- *The length of the final product.* A 500-word article obviously doesn't require as much preparation as one that's 5,000 words. The same for broadcast: getting a clip takes much less work than interviewing for a feature piece. However, there's a tendency, if the final item is short, to go after whatever has been reported before rather than come up with a new, perhaps better, approach.

WHAT COLOR SOCKS DID YOU WEAR ON YOUR FIRST HEIST?

The magnitude of research required for a book can be mind-boggling. The prolific author Gay Talese once said this about his research for the book, Honor Thy Father:

"I'm interested in the subject of organized crime in America. I had come to know, quite intimately, a family. By a family, I don't mean in the sense that the Attorney-General identifies families as comprising 400 machine-gun artists. I'm talking about a real family: father, mother, children, grandfathers, uncles, etc. I've come to know a family who in one way or another are on the other side of the law. I've come to know them so well that I am now in a position with veracity to think as they think, which is a lawless way to think.

"I have about 700 or 800 interviews. In the case of one person, who is a major subject in my book, I have gone through every month of his life—he's 38 years old—through interviews, from his first year in school as a first grader, right through

> *his first night in jail, right through his first crime,*
> *his first official crime, impressions that he has of his*
> *own misdemeanors, felonies, and those who exact*
> *judgment over him. I've really covered this man's*
> *life through interviews. The son is somewhat around*
> *my own age, and I know this man very, very well,*
> *certainly know him better than his wife does. In*
> *many ways, I could tell his wife things about him."*

BONE UP

"All too often, journalists start an interview armed only with a handful of questions scribbled in their notebooks," the Poynter Institute says. "Take time, however short, to bone up on your subject or the topic you'll be discussing."

When former *New York Times* reporter Mirta Ojito interviews experts, "I try to know almost as much as they do about their subject, so it seems we are 'chatting.'" A. J. Liebling, a legendary writer for *The New Yorker,* landed an interview with the notoriously tight-lipped jockey Willie Shoemaker. He opened with a single question: "Why do you ride with one stirrup higher than the other?" Impressed by Liebling's knowledge, Shoemaker opened up.

Educate yourself both about the topic about to be discussed, and about the person. For example, if you're going to interview a politician about climate change, assess how knowledgeable you are on the topic; how much you know about the politician and their party's stance on the issue; what the opposition critics are saying about climate change; and look into recent and relevant scientific and political developments.

Interviewees often tell me they're appalled by the lack of knowledge some interviewers display. "They use the interview with me as their research," one said, "and expect me to do their homework for them."

Would you arrive at a job interview knowing little or nothing about the company you hope will hire you? Of course not. But some journalists will engage in an interview with an expert having limited or no knowledge of the topic. Small wonder some interviewees get miffed.

The comedian Jerry Lewis said it was easy to tell if a journalist hadn't done any homework: "The first question they ask is, 'So, Jerry, what brings you to town?' I have no patience for that kind of person. He's lazy, he doesn't like his job, he doesn't like you. And what upsets me the most is that there's a kid out there who would give his eye teeth to have his job. I say to him, 'Look, you've got just two minutes, and at the end of those two minutes I'm walking out of here because you're a jerk, you're obviously not prepared, and you're wasting my time.' And then the guy goes away and writes what a jerk *I* am."

By the way, the interviewer who elicited that story, CBC broadcaster Jim Wright, found Lewis to be "totally professional: he was intelligent, cooperative and attentive."

One caveat: don't show off your knowledge. Instead of asking questions to elicit answers from the guest, some interviewers provide the responses, or interrupt to add tidbits of information. It might be tempting to display the breadth of your research, but this almost always backfires. Invariably, you become the focus of the interview, which is the opposite of what you should want to transpire.

PREPARING QUESTIONS

Experienced interviewers know that no matter how carefully or cleverly they compose a list of questions for a guest, and decide the order in which to ask them, the actual interview will never unfold as planned. Invariably, something they imagined asking near the end is dealt with early on, as an offshoot of a different question.

It's next to impossible to control how an interview evolves. The purpose of preparing questions is not to draw a strict roadmap, a journalistic version of Waze, the popular road-directions app. It's to force yourself to think about the interview, what questions you might want to pose, how you'll word some of them and when you might ask them. This will heighten your understanding of how the interview might evolve, and it will likely relax you, as well.

An interview that lasts more than a few minutes is partly an intuitive process. While it's in progress, there are numerous decisions you have to make: Am I achieving my goals? How well are we communicating? Do I follow up on this answer? What's their body language telling me? Why am I feeling so nervous? Should I interrupt? What's my next question? Should I challenge that answer? And so on.

As Albert Einstein once said, "Intuition does not come to an unprepared mind." The more prepared you are, the more comfortable you'll be, and the more likely your intuition will work at an optimum level. When you combine these qualities with active, engaged listening, off-the-cuff questions—which often produce the best answers—will come more naturally.

For an in-depth feature interview or personality profile, consider major areas you'll want to explore. For example, family history (I like to start with a subject's grandparents); childhood; early influences; a mentor's role; specific successes; failures; turning points; present situation; a look ahead.

THE COST OF NOT KNOWING

Aside from bruising your ego, a noticeable lack of preparation can seriously take an interview off the rails.

This can even happen during the preliminary chat, about something as seemingly benign as the news, weather, or sports. For example, business executives or politicians might assume the interviewer is familiar with a current event, asking "What do you think about what's happening in..." as an icebreaker. If you have no idea what the person is talking about—and betray your ignorance—it might make the guest question your capability to conduct an intelligent exchange.

When I'm occasionally interviewed, this kind of disconnect makes me feel cautious. Concern that an interviewer is unprofessional or incompetent might cause me to feel nervous, like speeding down the autobahn with an inexperienced driver at the wheel. An obviously hapless interviewer might get the story wrong. This could result in the interviewee becoming more guarded, and less open.

Another possible reaction could be just the opposite. Convinced that the interviewer is a rookie or just not that smart, an interviewee might try to take control. Many of my students have reported that happening.

After I debriefed their experience, it seemed some interviewees realized they could steamroll over an inexperienced questioner.

A lack of basic information can also take an interview off-track, quickly. In a red-carpet interview at the 2015 Screen Actors Guild Awards, TNT correspondent Danielle Demski complimented Rashida Jones, of TV's *Parks and Recreation* fame, on her appearance: "You look like you've just come off an island or something. You're very tan, very tropical."

Like the Dalai Lama, Jones took the high road. The biracial actress, who is the daughter of renowned record producer Quincy Jones and actor Peggy Lipton, laughingly replied: "I mean, you know, I'm ethnic."

Not all are so kind.

Once again, I will use Larry King as an example. In November 2007, in a CNN interview with Jerry Seinfeld about his hit eponymous TV show, which ran from 1989 to 1998, King said, "You gave it up, right? They didn't cancel you?"

To which a stunned Seinfeld replied, "You're not aware of this?"

"No, I'm asking you," King said.

"You're under the impression I got cancelled?" Seinfeld continued, several times. "Is this still CNN? [*Seinfeld*] was the number one show on television. Do you know who I am, Larry?"

It was an awkward and unpleasant diversion from what should have been a substantive interview with a major star.

I don't want to give the impression that only people in front of a camera mess up. It's just that if an interview is recorded, it tends to exist online forever, sometimes making the punishment worse than the crime.

In fairness, there are interviewers who emulate Larry King's approach to preparation. One is Bob McCown, who ruled Toronto sports radio for decades.

"I've never gone into an interview with a list of questions," he once said. "I may have a direction that I want to go in, but my philosophy for a long time now has been that an interview is nothing more than a conversation, and a conversation is predicated on reacting, rather than planning.

"The key is not to be so caught up in your own role that you lose the ability to listen. Same thing with a list of questions. If you have them in front of you then, invariably, you're thinking about the next question rather than listening to the answer. The answer will give you the next question, and then that answer will give you the question after that. The subject's response always sets the road map for the interview.

"After it's over, someone might ask me, 'Did you get what you wanted?' and I'll say, 'Well, I didn't know what I wanted, but I got something. And it was a real conversation.' For me, that's the goal."

Podcaster Marc Maron is another interviewer who prefers not to prepare prior to an interview.

"I don't do a hell of a lot of research," he says. "I go on a sort of kindred-spirit bonding that preexists the interview, and just see what unfolds. I'm just looking for authentic engagement of some kind. Some people just want to answer questions, but a lot of times, all of a sudden you drift away, and you don't remember you're on the mic, and you're in something real. That, to me, is great."

This approach may work when the interviewer possesses quick, intellectual reflexes. Most of us, however, need to prepare.

A real conversation is, indeed, one of the most important goals for an interviewer. Can you get there without preparing? Some talented people can, but I think even they would do much better if they took the time and effort to prepare.

KEY TAKEAWAYS

- Preparation is critical to most successful interviews.
- Educate yourself, if necessary, on the subject area, not just the interviewee.
- Displaying ignorance of something you should have known can have lasting negative effects on you, especially if it's recorded and shared on social media.

TEN: WHAT ARE YOU WALKING INTO?

In 2008, the pro-labor periodical *This Magazine* sent me to interview Ken Lewenza, who had just been elected head of the Canadian Auto Workers. The CAW was one of the few organizations that bought ads in the low-budget magazine.

I assumed he knew all about the publication because his union helped to keep it afloat. That was a mistake, albeit a small one.

We chatted about some neutral subjects before getting down to the actual interview, for a Q&A column I wrote for each issue. Just as I was about to begin, and for no obvious reason other than ingrained discipline, I asked him, somewhat apologetically, whether he was familiar with *This Magazine*.

"I don't know anything about it," he said, revealing that he had no idea he was talking to a journalist from a labor-friendly publication. Of course, this likely would affect his approach to my questions. I quickly filled him in, and the interview went well.

If I had followed my own process—to take a moment during my preparation to assess what I might be walking into—I may have realized that the odds of a former auto assembly plant worker being aware of one of Canada's oldest, alternative, left-wing magazines were pretty small.

Here's what I ask myself before I interview someone for the first time:

- Is the interviewee likely friendly, hostile, neutral, or a combination of some or all of those potential traits?
- Is the person accustomed to being interviewed by the media, or fairly new at it?
- Do I have any intel on the person's attitude towards being interviewed? (This is especially important for interviews with prominent people.)
- Will the interviewee have any idea who I am, or the publication or broadcast outlet I work for?

Why do I do this quick scan? It's another aspect of preparation, an important one.

If I'm fairly certain the interviewee mistrusts the media, or the outfit I'm representing, I can steel myself for possible coldness or attacks and strategize how to react. That's preferable to being caught off-guard, and perhaps reacting badly to whatever comes my way. If I can't anticipate the reception I'm likely to receive, I'll prepare for the worst, just in case.

FOUR BASIC TYPES OF GUESTS

Decide whether your interviewee falls into one of the following categories. How will this affect your preparation?

1. *Someone who has done something considered positive.*
2. *Someone who has done something considered negative.*
3. *An expert or witness to a story.*
4. *Any combination of the above.*

WRONG ASSUMPTIONS

Many years ago, I was in New York City on assignment when the magazine I was working for told me to interview a vice president of news at a U.S. network. It was for an upcoming assignment about a controversial Canadian TV program that had been modeled on the American network's flagship current affairs show.

Unfortunately, there was a problem: the U.S. show wasn't broadcast in Ottawa, where I lived at the time. I had never seen it. I figured that because I'd be talking to a fellow journalist, it would get me through. I've never been more wrong.

My first mistake was to assume my guest was a journalist. Within seconds of meeting him, it became apparent he was a bureaucrat who treated someone like me with considerable suspicion and hostility. I had no previous experience with senior U.S. network TV executives. I have no idea whether they're all like this ice-cold man, but I'll never forget him.

He was aloof from the get-go, but once he realized I hadn't seen his program, he stopped talking, glowered at me and at the now-sweating PR guy who had brokered the interview, and refused to respond to anything more that I said. The three of us were in a small boardroom, and it was probably the most uncomfortable encounter of my long career.

I quickly found a way to wrap up, thanked the executive, who did not reply, and left.

In hindsight, I should have known I was walking into a potential minefield; but I was young and in NYC on my first assignment in that great city and had just come off a great interview with baseball star Rusty Staub, so I assumed I could wing the next one.

If I'd taken the time to come up with an explanation as to why I'd never seen the show (which I should have declared off the top) there might have been a better outcome. Or, I might have decided it was too risky to do the interview, although my magazine would not have been happy with that response. Anything would have been better than finding myself in such an uncomfortable and unproductive encounter.

The what-am-I-walking-into exercise I now do is not an exact science. I've been wrong in an expectation, and sometimes I've based my assessment on someone else's experience that wasn't accurate. Sometimes, the person didn't react the way I'd anticipated.

NOT AS PRICKLY AS ADVERTISED

The latter happened to me with the Pulitzer Prize-winning playwright Edward Albee, when I was on the board of directors of PEN Canada. I'd briefly met Albee at a PEN event some years prior and found him to be the crusty person I'd been warned about by other board members.

Several years later, Albee was returning to Toronto for another PEN fundraiser. Someone had to pick him up at the airport, but none of the other board members wanted to do it because of his prickly reputation. As a modestly successful playwright myself (to overstate), I figured the chance to spend time with one of America's greatest living writers (*Who's Afraid of Virginia Woolf?* et al.)

was worth whatever nastiness he was going to throw at me. I volunteered.

He turned out to be as nice as nice could be that day. Not only did we have a lively discussion about his plays in my car during the 45-minute drive from the airport to his hotel, he asked me about mine and seemed genuinely interested. I later read in *The New Yorker* that he'd softened somewhat over the years. Perhaps he was practicing his new persona on me.

I end with this anecdote to emphasize that we can never be sure how a person will react, but I also believe strongly that the more effort we put into anticipating what might lie ahead in an open and positive mindset, the greater the potential for a successful outcome.

WHO IS THE INTERVIEWEE TALKING TO?

On the surface, this might seem like a silly question. Obviously, it's you.

However, consider that the person may be thinking about people who are not in the room. A person representing a government department, a company or a non-profit organization may be more focused on appeasing their stakeholders than on you.

The first step is to recognize it's happening. Then, in a neutral tone, address it:

Q: It seems to me that your answers are directed to the people back at your office rather than to the general public (or a specific stakeholder group). Is that a fair comment?

KEY TAKEAWAYS

- Don't assume an interviewee knows who you are or why you're talking to them. Check in before the interview begins.
- Ask yourself what you might be walking into: a friendly, hostile, or neutral response, or a combination of more than one.
- Be aware that some guests are not talking to you but to a boss, stakeholder, etc. You might have to address that.

ELEVEN: **ROLE-PLAYING AND VISUALIZATION**

Prior to debating President Trump during the 2020 election campaign, former Vice President Joe Biden held mock debates. Bob Bauer, a former White House counsel, played the role of Trump. Although Bauer didn't dress the part, as some previous stand-ins for the president had done, he copied the president's style, energy, and tactics, to give Biden a sense of what might be coming his way.

Role-playing is not the sole reserve of politicians preparing for a tough encounter, such as a televised debate. Journalists sometimes find it helpful to employ this tactic before a high-profile interview, especially one they think might be confrontational.

It can be done by practicing beforehand with a colleague who assumes the part of the prospective interviewee, or by visualizing. The latter means thinking through how the interview might unfold.

Martha Mendoza, who has won two Pulitzer Prizes for journalism as a reporter for the Associated Press, advocates role-playing difficult interviews before they take place. In a 2018 article in *The Open Notebook (TON)*, a science journalism website, she described a time, in the late 1990s, when that didn't happen.

"She had just discovered what she hoped would be one of her first big scoops: she had documents proving that [some] U.S. Bureau of Land Management field officers had been rounding up wild horses and burros on BLM land and sending them for slaughter, while recording them as adopted," the website noted.

Mendoza decided to confront the officers at their headquarters. "The front door was locked but the side door was open, so she let herself in. Inside, she found all the officials she had hoped to interview, looking surprised. She dove right in, telling them about the documents she had and what they proved."

The officers denied her allegations and accused her of lying. They told her to get the hell out.

"It just kind of was a gotcha moment that didn't really tease out very much," she said.

Twenty-one years later, Mendoza told *TON* that if she could conduct the BLM interview again, there's a lot she would do differently.

"I would have role-played the whole thing," she said. That's something she and her team at AP now practice before difficult interviews. She told *TON* that she would have also "taken a long time letting them tell me about the program, asking lots of questions," to get the officials comfortable and to show she'd done her research.

The latter strategy has two primary benefits. By prompting them to talk about general information at the outset, instead of charging ahead with accusations, she would have likely been able to set an interview in motion.

When an interview has gone on for a period of time, it's harder to throw out the journalist following an unwelcomed question. As she pointed out, it also would have demonstrated how much she knew about the story, which could have had another effect: the officers might have respected or feared the extent of her knowledge.

The Open Notebook says that Rob Cribb, an award-winning investigative reporter for *The Toronto Star*, uses a tactic similar to Mendoza's. Before sitting down with an important source, he creates a flowchart, starting with his first question and mapping out every possible answer and his follow-up questions. Then he meets with his editor and they act out different routes through the chart. It's a lot of work, but after he's done this, Cribb says he's supremely well-prepared, not just for the interview but also for writing the story.

LIKE CHESS

Visualizing how the interview might unfold is easier than role-playing, as it doesn't require anything but your experience and imagination. This is how veteran CBC TV documentary maker Terence McKenna applies this technique, prior to a tough encounter:

"I approach these confrontational or aggressive interviews a lot like a chess game, planning them out a great deal," he said. "The first thing I do is make a list of questions. Then I try to really put myself in their skin and think how they will answer. I would block an interview out, saying, if I ask this question, they will likely say that, in which case I can come to a follow-up question. Based on the answers, you're offered a choice of which way you can go. And then it becomes a game, a certain role-playing. You really try to think of how they think, of what their answers will be.

"In other words, in a real confrontational situation, it's a game of sort of pushing a man into a room where there are four doors. And you figure out which door he's most likely to go through and you try to close off the doors you don't want him to go through in the way you phrase your question. And then you push him into a room with three doors, then two and one, if you know what I mean. In the way you approach, you try and keep him on your game plan so that he can't escape the points that you want to establish, that you want to have him answer. In an interview like that, I would spend hours thinking about what he could say, what I could say in response, and redraft my questions to do that."

Elite chess players also practise visualization. As thechessworld.com says, "This ability allows a chess player to calculate tactics precisely multiple moves ahead and, most importantly, it makes it possible to picture and evaluate the final position correctly."

Professional golfers say that if you visualize where a shot is heading, the chance of it getting there increases considerably. "Tiger Woods often talks about seeing the shot before he hits it," Golf Channel notes.

American swimmer Michael Phelps, who won a record total of 28 medals at five Olympic Games, used visualization from an early age. "When I would visualize," Phelps says, "it would be what you want it to be, what you don't want it to be, what it could be. You are always ready for whatever comes your way."

His longtime coach Bob Bowman says, "By the time Michael got up on the blocks to swim in the World Championships or Olympics, he'd swum that race hundreds of times in his mind."

Whether to role-play or visualize is a personal decision. Many journalists don't subscribe to either approach and do perfectly well nonetheless. Personally, I like a mixture of rehearsal and spontaneity, with emphasis on the latter.

I begin by writing down the major areas I need to cover, producing a sort of blueprint. That leads to the next step, which is jotting down some questions for each section, in point form, in roughly the order in which I think they'll come up.

I'll imagine how the interview might transpire. I used to plot moves and countermoves with the cunning of a jealous lover. Now it's casual, more to prepare than to defend. Rather than fixating on how to "win," my goal is to find the best questions, and the strategies to ask them. However, accomplishing that in an adversarial situation can require intricate planning and foresight.

While mapping out the questions, key information and strategies emerge. How many questions do I have? What points are missing, weak, unprovable, or likely to be challenged? Where am I vulnerable to attack? Why? How will I respond? What questions require careful wording? Where are the major transitions? What themes are emerging as the strongest? How prepared and confident am I?

This process is not linear and clinical. It's not done to ordain certain responses. It's much more fluid than that, a means whereby I become familiar with the subject matter, the guest, and my own feelings and ideas, all at the same time.

Depending on the circumstances, I'll review questions and possible answers in detail, but more often than not, the greatest benefit of the imaginative process is to relax me. Rather than venturing toward the unknown, it helps me feel more connected and comfortable with what lies ahead.

CONFRONTATIONAL AND EMOTIONALLY CHARGED INTERVIEWS

For confrontational or accountability interviews, my inclination is to follow McKenna's paradigm: to visualize how I will word the toughest questions, when I'll ask them and what answers I can anticipate. It's wise to prepare both for truthful responses, and for evasive or otherwise unhelpful ones. If the latter happens, what will I do?

I also assess the quality of my research. Do I have the information, documents, or other relevant material required, in case the interviewee challenges the veracity of what I'm saying or alleging?

A few decades ago, a friend of mine interviewed Canadian-born singer Paul Anka in his home in Carmel, California.

"He was a scary man, a martinet with the people around him," the writer said. "When I was interviewing him about the old days, about when he wrote 'Diana' [his first big hit at age 15], there was no problem. He loved it. But I wanted to talk to him about the stories that he had Mob connections. I said, 'Since you have talked about your delight in writing [the iconic song] 'My Way' for Sinatra, and the words Sinatra and Vegas connote the Mob to the average reader, how do you feel when your career has that aura to it?'

"He said, 'It's ridiculous,' with reptilian speed. When he snapped the word 'ridiculous' in a low voice, it was like a gun cocked. I changed the topic."

While it took moxie to ask Anka, in his home, a question like that, in hindsight it was probably not a good idea unless the writer had evidence that the statement was accurate. He didn't.

When Anka published his 2013 autobiography, aptly titled *My Way*, he mentioned the presence of the Mafia in the circles in which he traveled. "[He] admits he himself had a cozy relationship with the boys," the *Daily News* said in a review of the book. "No one tried to take him over, to run him, but they were friendly. He says he felt just a little more secure when the guys were around, but Sinatra was 'fascinated' with the Mafia."

Perhaps the writer could have started by talking about Sinatra's relationship with organized criminals, a contention it's unlikely Anka would have denied. Then he could have asked the singer whether he was ever around these characters himself, either in Sinatra's company or by hanging out in places such as Las Vegas. That likely would also have elicited a "yes." The next chess move would have been to ask whether he had ever been linked to the Mafia, as a result of his proximity to Sinatra.

DON'T BE BULLIED INTO ATTACKING

I caution you to resist being bullied or intimidated by editors or other senior media personnel into "going after" an interviewee. If you hear them say something along the lines of, "I want you to nail that guy" on such-and-such a topic, don't agree to do it, unless you can back up the allegations.

There are many pitfalls: it's unethical to sling mud without proof; you might lose future access to an important source; the interview could be terminated prematurely; and, in some cases, you could suffer reputational damage.

If an unproven allegation is broadcast or published, you might even be sued.

There is a world of difference between knowing something to be true and proving it. Even if you're certain that what you're about to allege is accurate, take a moment to ask if you could defend it in a court of law. However, don't be afraid to challenge an interviewee on a matter that couldn't possibly result in court action. (I've been shocked at the petty things some interviewees threatened to sue over.)

It's important for interviewers, especially journalists, to be aware of the laws governing slander, libel, and defamation. There are numerous helpful resources online, especially at The Poynter Institute (www.poynter.org).

I also take extra time to prepare for interviews that may involve deeply emotional or painful memories. For an interview with a woman who had been raped on a business trip in Texas, I spent a great deal of time visualizing how I would begin our discussion, the wording I would use when we started to talk about the assault, and how I'd react if she found the conversation too painful or needed a break. (I would immediately give her the option to end the interview.)

You don't want to blurt out upsetting wording during the interview because you're nervous about the topic.

I once worked with a radio host who struggled with emotional interviews. I learned this early on when we did an item about a considerably short male and quite a tall woman. My host managed to insult them both about their physical stature because he was so uncomfortable probing their feelings.

It's also critical to be in the right psychological state of mind. If you visualize the interview, imagine it unfolding in a positive way. This applies to areas of the interview that might be fraught with conflict. Face that possibility and devise a plan in which there's a successful outcome.

As Maxwell Maltz, the author of *The New Psycho-Cybernetics* wrote, "A human being always acts and feels and performs in accordance with what he imagines to be true about himself and his environment. For imagination sets the goal 'picture,' which our automatic mechanism works on. We act, or fail to act, not because of 'will,' as is so commonly believed, but because of imagination."

KEY TAKEAWAYS

- Consider visualizing challenging interviews.
- Assess the quality of your research before conducting an accountability or confrontational interview.
- Spend extra time preparing for an interview about a highly emotional or traumatic event.

TWELVE: **BE CONVERSATIONAL**

A few years ago, I was hired to salvage a book project gone awry. It was a celebration of the 100th anniversary of an amazing U.S. company. The original writer, who'd just retired as a lifelong newspaper journalist, hadn't been able to produce more than one chapter of a draft that met the client's expectations, despite working on the project for about a year.

When I first met the company's CEO, a no-nonsense guy with a clear but demanding approach, he imposed one condition when I said I'd need to re-interview him. (The original writer had spent considerable time with the CEO.)

"No chitchat," he said, emphatically. "The last guy had no idea what he was doing. He wasted my time."

I knew exactly what he meant because I'd read transcripts of their conversations. They were rambling, unfocused discussions that, I thought, revealed how much the writer wanted to show off his intellectual skills.

The writer, indeed, was smart. But he had a deep-seated need to impress and, in doing so, there was no real purpose to the interviews. The exchanges produced almost no quotes I could use. For example, at one point the CEO mentioned his company had an office in Peru. The interviewer's response? He talked at length about a presentation his wife, an academic, had made at a conference in Peru years earlier.

He didn't understand his job was to get the interviewee talking, then (verbally) step out of the way. Nor was he aware that although an interview should be conducted in a conversational style, it should not be a random conversation. Everything the interviewer discusses with the guest should have a purpose, even if the topics appear to be just idle chatter.

Being conversational, rather than reciting a list of questions (like a telemarketer), is critical to success. Being a good conversationalist is also helpful.

A PAS DE DEUX

For interviews in which you're trying to elicit information (rather than, say, holding an audience's interest by getting an interesting person to talk in an interesting way), it might be helpful to keep in mind this comment by TV journalist Warner Troyer. An interview, he said, "bears about as much relationship to a conversation as walking across the street has to do with a *pas de deux* [in ballet]."

I think that's true for most interviews. On a TV talk show, the goal is to have a riveting conversation. One of the masters of this art is Dick Cavett, long retired, but his work is readily available on YouTube. He had his own show on ABC from 1968 to 1974.

Cavett recalls the advice TV host Jack Paar gave him. "He said, 'Hey kid, don't do interviews.' I thought, 'Did I hear you right? Am I supposed to read to the guests?' he said, 'No, no, no. I mean interviews. Q and A. [Instead], make it a conversation." Few did that better than Cavett.

The Cavett-style interview requires a host to inspire, provoke and, sometimes, challenge. In December 1971, he had two of America's most famous and feistiest writers, Norman Mailer and Gore Vidal, on his show together. They didn't like each other and loved to spar in public. At one point, Mailer was annoyed with Cavett and dismissed him by saying: "Why don't you look at your question sheet and ask a question?" To which Cavett replied: "Why don't you fold it five ways and put it where the moon don't shine?" The audience convulsed with laughter.

Few of us have Cavett's intellectual prowess (which he once defined as having actually read a guest's book) or his quick wit. But the more we educate ourselves, the more likely we are to hold our own with an interesting guest. As NPR's celebrated interviewer Terry Gross pointed out to *The New York Times* in 2018, a good interviewer is "somebody who is fun to talk to."

WE ALL MAKE MISTAKES

I doubt there's an interviewer who didn't make a slew of mistakes in their early days. It's inevitable you'll mess up at the start of your career. One method to help improve your interviewing style is to deconstruct your interviews: what worked, what didn't, what research was lacking, etc. It can take courage at times to face what went wrong in an unsuccessful interview, but it's one of the best ways to improve over time.

Be kind to yourself when you make mistakes, especially when starting out. It's similar to learning how to drive a car. You might have gone to driver's ed (journalism school), but you don't really learn how to drive until you're behind the wheel alone, making instantaneous decisions, just as you have to do during an interview.

As Henry Ford said, "The only real mistake is the one from which we learn nothing."

KEY TAKEAWAYS

- Don't engage in idle chitchat with a guest. Everything you say or do should have a purpose and contribute to you achieving your goals.
- Study how to be an effective conversationalist.
- Accept that you will make mistakes. Try to learn from them.

THIRTEEN: **IT'S OKAY TO BE SHY**

On a modest book tour for *Asking Questions*, I was interviewed on CBC Radio's flagship network current affairs program, *Morningside*. As I left the studio, a producer told me I had a call from a listener.

The caller was a retired print journalist and editor of some renown. He was the archetypal gruff-sounding guy whose hard exterior belied a kind heart. After telling me his name, he said this: "When I heard you introduced, I thought, I've never heard of this guy. Why in God's name should I listen to anything he has to say about interviewing? But then, early on, you said that many journalists are actually shy, although a lot of them pretend they're not. When you said that, I realized you probably knew what you were talking about because I know that's true. That's why I called you. Just to say that. Goodbye."

I'm not identifying him because I'm not sure I remember who it was (there are a couple of contenders), but it's notable that this man made an effort to reach me to underline a point that mattered to him. Perhaps he was shy (I didn't have a chance to ask him) and had never really admitted it to his colleagues. Or perhaps, as a veteran writer and editor, he had seen enough journalists come and go to know the truth—not all of us are extroverts.

U.S. journalist Jen Retter eloquently made this point in a 2013 post on the blog *Ninja Journalism*. "When I say I'm a reporter, the looks I get are priceless. When people see this soft-spoken, high-voiced young woman who routinely spends entire evenings reading and sipping coffee, they never guess I spend my 8-to-5s (and more) in a position typically portrayed on TV as gutsy. Despite the fact that 'reserved' and 'reporter' don't sound like they go together in the (fictional) media's perception of the world, I've found that the two correlate quite well in the real world. It is highly possible to prefer smaller groups, alone time, and quiet—and be a successful reporter."

Retter notes that her "introversion helps me to find the story in the mess. Introverts are listeners. When I'm in a conversation, I'm not caught up in trying to get my point of view in or draw attention to myself. I pay attention. I read people well. That's how I find stories— I listen intently, and I catch key points mid-interview to use as my angle."

She says this also helps to channel her empathy. "When your heart aches, whom do you call: the bar-hopper who can fill you in on the latest Kardashian gossip or the listener who will hear what you have to say for as long as it takes you to get it out? My listen-first approach sets me up to be the person my friends come to for comfort. In this respect, the tough stories are the ones an introvert can master."

This is not to say, by any means, that extroverts aren't good journalists or that they lack listening skills or empathy. I consider myself an extrovert who sometimes slips into introversion. Both aspects of my character help me talk to people in whatever circumstances arise.

I mention shyness because I find students and new journalists who perceive themselves as shy often ask whether it's a deterrent. The extroverts never wonder whether being outgoing is a liability.

WHAT IF I'M YOUNG AND HAVE A HIGH VOICE?

I'm often asked by people who believe they have a high-sounding voice, whether this is a problem. It might exclude you from some broadcast work, I say truthfully (although Barbara Walters is ample proof that an unusual voice doesn't have to be an impediment in broadcasting), but not print.

I don't think many interviewers take voice lessons to lower their register (although it can help), so my advice is: try to accept your voice. It's almost never as problematic as you perceive it to be. Instead, focus on research and questions. Perhaps an interviewee will underestimate you because of your voice. It's good to be underestimated because the interviewee might let down their guard.

As for your age, you can't do anything about that. What you can do is make sure you're as prepared as possible. Once an interview starts, if the interviewee realizes you know what you're doing, age and voice tend to become irrelevant.

KEY TAKEAWAYS

- Many journalists are shy. It can be an asset, not a detriment.
- Accept your voice, no matter how you think it sounds.
- You can't change your age, how you look, or your experience, but you can research and prepare to a point that makes those characteristics inconsequential.

FOURTEEN: ASKING A PERSON'S AGE

If my students are any indication, many young interviewers feel uncomfortable asking an interviewee for their age. They say it's too personal a question.

It's not. There are many valid reasons for needing a person's age (or, at least, an approximate) in a story.

Although the Internet has made it easier to determine how old a person is, there are numerous instances when you have to ask. Of course, not everyone is comfortable answering. When that happens, you need to be able to explain why their age is important to the story.

Here are a few points to raise:

- It gives readers a sense of what major events have shaped an interviewee's life and way of thinking. For example, a 30-year-old American in 2020 was about 10 when 9/11 happened; a 50-year-old might have had a parent who fought in the Vietnam War; a 70-year-old might have had parents who served in World War II, and so on.

- A person's age also offers a sense of their cultural influences, such as music, film, and social media, that could play a role in their observations and opinions. A 30-year-old might cite Drake as a musical icon while the 50-year-old might relate more to Madonna or Bruce Springsteen. (It's important to note that influences can transcend generations.) Someone who grew up before social media has been shaped by different factors than a person who has always had access to the Internet and a smartphone.

- It can differentiate the person from someone with the same name but of a significantly different age. I've sometimes seen a person's age and realized it was not the person I was looking for.
- It can help readers know whether the person is at the starting point of something or in their later years. A 40-year-old athlete, as one example, is at a much different stage in their career than a 17-year-old.

Knowing a person's age can be of great benefit to an interviewer; it can help you better understand and connect with an interviewee. When teaching, I try to keep in mind, for example, that referencing the Beatles to my students might not be useful.

To help me remember that, I think back to The Open Championship of 2014, which was held at the Royal Liverpool Golf Club in Merseyside, England, about 10 miles from where the Fab Four started out. Many of the golfers, including stars Rory McIlroy and Bubba Watson, couldn't name the four lads. Rather than saying *tsk tsk*, someone my age needs to understand that we might not be able to name the top rappers of the 2000s.

Sometimes an approximate age is revealed in a published story—for example, when Linden MacIntyre retired as one of the hosts of CBC TV's *the fifth estate*, a May 2014 article in *The Globe and Mail* didn't mention his age, but noted he was celebrating "50 years as a journalist this month." Using an indirect reference may not provide enough information. A 70-year-old (MacIntyre was about to turn 71 at the time) is quite different, say, from an 80-year-old, which he very well could have been, if he had started in journalism later in life.

The Internet can be a helpful tool to estimate a person's age. For example, it's possible to conclude, perhaps by seeing a person's work history and year of graduation from university on LinkedIn, approximately how old they are.

I used to ask interviewees for their exact date of birth so I'd know their age when my story was published (back in the day that could be many months after our last interview), but fear of identity theft has made many people leery about sharing such specific personal information. In those cases, I ask whether their current age is likely to change in the next few months.

As a final effort, a family member or friend can provide the information, or at least an educated guess. The few times I've asked this, I've had moderate success, with some refusals and some gleeful divulgences.

KEY TAKEAWAYS

- A person's age is often an important detail to acquire.
- If the interviewee won't tell you, use the Internet or other resources (friends/family) to find it out.
- Don't ask for the exact year and date of birth. Many people fear this information could be used by identity thieves.

FIFTEEN: **WE'RE NOT THE POLICE**

How can I control the interview? How can I make the person admit to what they did? How can I force them to answer me?

These are some of the questions I'm often asked. My answer to each is always the same: you can't. It's important to understand this critical, and limiting, aspect of your role.

The only person you can control is yourself. You can attempt to guide an interview along a certain path, but there's no guarantee it will work. Nor should you threaten or otherwise try to bully an interviewee into answering.

Interviewees are under no legal obligation to answer you. There could be moral, ethical, professional, societal, or other influences that could persuade them to provide a response (be it honest and accurate or not). But, ultimately, they can just refuse.

A senior CBC executive producer used to say to his crew of documentary makers that asking a question mattered the most, not whether it elicited an amazing or gotcha response or no comment whatsoever. In fact, no answer is, indeed, an answer.

If you ask your partner where they spent the evening and they serve up a vague explanation or change the subject and create a distraction that allows the question to linger unanswered, that's quite a telling response.

In other words, you don't need the interviewee to break down and congratulate you on how incisive your question is before blubbering out an admission of some degree of wrongdoing.

That rarely happens.

It also doesn't mean you accept a non-response and move on. I have a personal rule that I will ask something three times at the most before moving on to my next inquiry. I might tinker with the wording each time, but if nothing is forthcoming, I won't belabor it after those three attempts.

A possible strategy is to ask, nicely in most cases, why the person is refusing to answer. "I'm just wondering why you don't seem to want to answer this question," could be a way of stating it. Or "Is there something about this question that's making you uncomfortable?" or words to that effect. Your tone, of course, is critical. It should be calm, not aggressive or confrontational.

GIVE THEM A REASON

An interviewer should always have a reason as to why someone should talk to them. Many assume that being a journalist is justification enough. It's not. Even major TV programs, such as *60 Minutes* or *the fifth estate*, or prominent newspapers, such as *The New York Times* or *The Globe and Mail*, can't coerce a person into talking if they don't want to or have been advised against it.

It's more persuasive to explain why they should agree to an interview. Here are some possibilities:

- No one can tell your story better than you.

- You can help others by saying what you understand to have happened.
- You can influence/change a law/rule by telling your story (for example, if a child was killed by a car on a busy street, her story might help convince the city to install a traffic light).
- You can set the record straight.
- You can give voice to a loved one, perhaps, who can no longer speak for themselves.
- You can do the right thing.
- We'll be doing the story with or without you.
- The optics will be better for you, or your organization, if you address this issue, rather than ignore it.

AMBUSH INTERVIEWS

There is one type of interview that comes close to what the authorities sometimes do when investigating a person. Often called an "ambush" or "jump interview," it's an unscheduled interaction with someone who is likely under a cloud of suspicion and has refused to grant an interview, despite numerous requests.

The ambush interview is thought to have been popularized by Mike Wallace early in his career. In a 2013 online article, *60 Minutes* admitted that Wallace "was famous for ambushing conmen and crooks, chasing them down with camera crews and a list of tough questions. It's an interview method that's used sparingly these days."

In a 2006 interview with media journalist Howard Kurtz, Wallace confessed "that there was more heat than light that came out of [ambush encounters]. "We weren't getting a lot of information from those so-called ambushes. So we quit. I have no doubt what we started has become a plague."

At some point (I don't know when), the CBC began requiring programs to get permission from their Journalism Standards and Practices office before and after conducting what Bob McKeown, senior host of *the fifth estate,* calls (with a twinkle in his voice) "spontaneous interactions."

McKeown has done a few of these during his long career, including a hidden-camera encounter in 2005 with David Frost, a hockey coach and agent who had allegedly been the target of an attempted contract murder hit orchestrated by a player he once coached as a 10-year-old, former NHLer Mike Danton. Danton was sentenced to seven-and-a-half years in prison for the scheme.

The fifth estate had obtained recordings of a conversation Frost had with Danton while he was in jail for the crime. Frost implored the 23-year-old to tell psychiatrists that an abusive childhood triggered the murder plot.

At the end of the conversation, Frost asked, "Okay, you love me?"

"Yeah," Danton said.

"Say it," Frost demanded.

"I love you."

Frost had declined numerous requests for an interview with *the fifth estate,* so McKeown obtained permission to approach him at a minor hockey rink in Peterborough, Ontario. A colleague had a camera hidden in her ball-cap. Although Frost denied all allegations presented to him, the interaction added a necessary element to the program's documentary on the bizarre relationship between the two men, entitled "Rogue Agent."

"He knew who I was and seemed only too happy to talk to us," McKeown says. "With Frost, and anyone else I interview, I try to be respectful no matter what they might have been accused of. That, to me, is the key as to how to do these encounters. I talked to Wayne Williams [the alleged Atlanta child murderer] the same way I would anyone else. There was a time when swaggering and being belligerent was the norm. Not so much anymore. I try to give people the leeway to explain themselves as well as possible."

GOING UNDERCOVER AND HIDDEN CAMERAS

A few brave journalists have gone undercover to expose wrongdoing. Antonio Salas (a pseudonym) spent years posing as the webmaster for feared terrorist, Carlos the Jackal, which exposed human trafficking, among other crimes.

Other examples include feminist Gloria Steinem who, in 1963, spent a month undercover for *Show* magazine working as a bunny at New York's Playboy Club, to reveal its working conditions. (She later co-founded *Ms.* magazine.)

Hidden cameras and fake credential often are employed during undercover assignments. These practices, however, suffered a blow in the 1990s when the North Carolina-based Food Lion grocery chain sued ABC's *Primetime Live*. The TV segment alleged that "Food Lion's meat department...required employees to engage in unsafe, unhealthy, or illegal practices, including selling old meat that was washed with bleach to kill odor, selling cheese that had been gnawed by rats and working off the time clock," the Reporters Committee for Freedom of the Press reported.

The problem for ABC was that two *Primetime* producers unearthed these unsafe practices after they were hired by Food Lion under misleading pretenses. They had submitted job applications "with false references, misrepresenting their educational and employment experiences on their résumés and omitting their current employment with the network. Each worked undercover for one or two weeks at the store, using hidden cameras to secretly record employees treating, wrapping, and labeling meat, cleaning machinery, and discussing meat-department practices." Food Lion originally won a $5.5-million settlement in the case but, after appeals, it was reduced to just two dollars.

It seems to me that the exposé justified the means; however, the *Columbia Journalism Review* cautioned that "the fallout [from Food Lion v. ABC] may not be limited to the case at hand. During the Food Lion controversy, Marvin Kalb of Harvard's Shorenstein Center worried that widespread use of deception 'demeans journalism and damages badly the journalist and the public.'

"This is not a theoretical problem. In announcing the verdict in the Food Lion case, the jury foreman told ABC, 'You didn't have boundaries when you started this investigation. You kept pushing on the edges and pushing on the edges. It was too extensive and fraudulent.'"

I'm in no way advocating that journalists should abandon the use of hidden cameras, undercover investigations or "spontaneous interactions." Rather, I echo the *CJR*'s concern that they should only be used to further the understanding of a story and that "the gimmick is not all there is."

In 1995, the Poynter Institute's Bob Steele agreed. He argued that the use of deception and hidden cameras is appropriate, "when the information obtained is of profound importance. It must be of vital public interest, such as revealing great 'system failure' at the top levels, or it must prevent profound harm to individuals [or] when all other alternatives for obtaining the same information have been exhausted."

The first of Steele's requirements is subjective, of course, although I sense most of us know how important a story's findings will likely turn out to be. If I have any concern, it's that less experienced journalists, imbued by a gung-ho "let's go get 'em" approach, might employ these tactics rashly and without the approval or oversight of senior colleagues. No one wants to see an important story quashed or derailed because the proper steps weren't followed.

KEY TAKEAWAYS

- You should always have a reason why an interviewee should talk to you.
- Ambush interviews are rarely used anymore but can be effective in special circumstances.
- Be careful when going undercover that any deception you might employ could come back to discredit you or your story.

SIXTEEN: **TRANSITIONING TO PERFORMANCE MODE**

One of my favorite sports interviewees was Dave Cutler, the incredible field goal kicker for the Edmonton Eskimos (now the Edmonton Elks, as of 2021) of the Canadian Football League. Cutler was an accomplished athlete who helped his team, over a 16-year career, win six Grey Cup championships. He was also funny and insightful.

I almost always learn something from each interview, and Cutler taught me several helpful things I later used in my practice.

In one of our conversations, he spoke about how he had difficulty, when he started out, transitioning from what he called "sideline mode" to "performance mode." During a game, he spent almost all of the time trying to keep his teammates loose by being funny. On several occasions, of course, he would be called on to kick a field goal; sometimes, the outcome of the game depended on the accuracy of his right foot.

"At first, I would run onto the field in the most direct path I could take," he said, "which was often a diagonal towards the ball. After a while, however, I started to realize I was having trouble transitioning from sideline mode, where I tried to keep everyone laughing, to performance mode. One day, I decide to enter the field by only running along the straight lines marked throughout the field, no matter where the ball was placed. My job was to kick the ball on a linear path, so that action made sense to me. It also helped condition me, mentally, to go from one mode to the other."

I realized that I, too, had trouble at times transitioning from whatever I was doing, such as writing or editing, to "interviewing mode." So, I took a page out of the athletic playbook and incorporated what many elite athletes had told me they do: pick a word of phrase to help send the right message to the brain prior to, say, trying to clear the bar in a high jump or throwing a javelin.

I picked a scene from the film *All That Jazz,* about choreographer Bob Fosse. In the movie, the Fosse character, played by Roy Scheider, looks at a mirror before heading into a new day, despite not feeling well, and says, "It's showtime." It reminded me that no matter how I felt, I had to put all else behind and perform.

There were times when I had to conduct an interview, teach a class, or lead an all-day training seminar while exhausted, fighting a cold or other illness and said "It's showtime" just before the activity started. On many occasions, I was able to do my job, functioned well and, by the end of the day, I often actually felt better. I don't want to get all metaphysical about this, but I believe sending this message to myself beforehand helped.

Cutler also told me he had studied the book *Zen in the Art of Archery*, by the German philosopher Eugen Herrigel, as it seemed to relate to what he did for a living—send a projectile towards a target under pressure. My version of this was to read as much about human behavior as I could. He also kept a journal on every kick he ever made, both in practice and in a game. Would that I had done the same about every interview I'd ever conducted. Imagine how much I would have learned about how I conducted my craft.

KEY TAKEAWAYS

- Consider adopting a phrase or some other prompt that helps prepare you for an upcoming interview or performance.
- Interviewees can often teach us, if we are open to what they have to offer.
- Deconstruct, if you can, each interview to see what worked and what didn't.

SEVENTEEN: INVASIVE PERSONAL QUESTIONS AND SEXISM

During a 2012 promotional interview for *The Avengers*, Jerry Penacoli, a host of the syndicated U.S. entertainment program *Extra*, asked Scarlett Johansson about the skin-tight costume she wore in the role of the Black Widow.

"Were you able to wear undergarments—" he began, until Johansson cut him off.

"You're like the fifth person that's asked me that. What's going on? Since when did people start asking each other in interviews about their underwear?"

Penacoli tried to justify his question, but with little success.

"To ask somebody what kind of underpants they're wearing?" Johansson questioned. "What kind of interview is this?"

Earlier in the tour, the actress had to endure a similar unsettling query. Her costar, Robert Downey Jr., was asked by a female reporter about anything he might have learned from playing Iron Man; the reporter then turned to Johansson: "To get into shape for Black Widow, did you have anything special to do in terms of the diet? Like, did you have to eat any specific food, or that sort of thing?"

"How come you get the really interesting existential question, and I get the like, 'rabbit food' question?"

Johansson complained to Downey Jr. She was obviously not happy about being on the receiving end of questions she felt were only asked of female stars.

Neither was singer Ariana Grande pleased during a November 2015 interview on Los Angeles's Power 106 radio station. The hosts asked her a series of idiotic questions, topped by this one: "If you could use makeup or your phone one last time, what would you pick?"

"Is this what you think girls have trouble choosing between?" she testily replied.

When finally asked a serious question, about what she would like to see changed in the world, she threw some shade at the hosts: "Judgment, intolerance, meanness, double standards, misogyny, racism, sexism. You know, all that shit. There's lots we've got to get started on. We've got work to do. We'll start with you, though."

Any stroll through YouTube will unearth numerous other cringeworthy interviews displaying flagrant sexism, almost all aimed at female performers. Emma Watson, as one example, was attacked for having posed semi-topless for a *Vanity Fair* photoshoot while having the audacity to call herself a feminist. "I really don't know what my tits have to do with it," she later said.

Not all who are subjected to these types of questions are female, though. On February 10, 1993, Oprah Winfrey landed a one-on-one interview with Michael Jackson, the first he'd granted in 14 years. The TV audience of 90 million was the largest in history for an interview. Oprah covered many controversial topics, but one stood out.

OW: "I'm going to ask you this and it's embarrassing for me to ask you, but I'm going to ask you anyway: are you a virgin?"

MJ: "I'm a gentleman. That's something that's private,

that shouldn't be spoken about openly. You can call me old-fashioned if you want, but to me that's very personal."

Should she have posed such an intrusive question? Sixteen years later, she said she knew it was something audiences had wanted to know. "There was this sort of mystery about him. At the same time, he's holding his crotch and wants to rock with us all night [but] we don't know who he's rocking with. That's what you really want to know."

I think if you have to apologize for asking a question, such as Oprah did by admitting her embarrassment, then you shouldn't ask it. But that was maybe just her nervousness seeping out.

Is it fair to ask a man in his mid-30s whether he's had intercourse? I don't believe I could have done it, but I recognize it was something many people likely had wondered about Jackson. He deflected it well, though, and she didn't harvest a bombshell response.

The Oprah question opens the door to what I consider to be the bottom line when considering asking about matters of sex or sexuality: is the question relevant? I'm guessing no one cared what Robert Downey Jr. wore underneath his Iron Man costume, but a lot of "boys" likely drooled at the possibility Scarlett Johansson went commando under hers. Was it relevant? Absolutely not.

Is it relevant to pose reasonable weight loss and diet questions to a woman who takes on a superhero character, as was asked of Anne Hathaway about her Catwoman role? My sense is yes, just as it was pertinent to talk to Christian Bale about the 63 pounds he lost to make *The Machinist*. It becomes problematic, however, when these kinds of questions are directed only at women.

It also depends on the way they're presented. If there's any type of apparent, underlying salaciousness, I don't think the question should be asked unless you work for an outlet that's known to focus on such matters (Howard Stern, come on down). If it's posed as a serious matter that could elicit an interesting and pertinent response, there should not be a problem.

Here's a test to consider during your prep: if the woman challenges you as to why you want to know something, and you have no reasonable answer, don't ask it.

SHOULD MALE JOURNALISTS BE ALLOWED TO INTERVIEW FEMALE CELEBRITIES IN GLOSSY MAGAZINES?

A 2017 article in The Guardian *by Hadley Freeman examined this question, asked of her by a reader. The following is part of her response.*

"I have been a connoisseur of male journalists' interviews with female celebrities for several decades now, collecting them as pieces of evidence for my soon-to-be published epic tome, The Male Ego: Beyond Belief. *My interest was first piqued by an interview fellow 90s kids might remember, Rich Cohen's 1995 profile of Alicia Silverstone in* Rolling Stone, *which opened with the promising sentence, 'Alicia Silverstone is a kittenish 18-year-old movie star whom lots of men want to sleep with…She has the brand-new look of a still-wet painting—touch her and she'll smudge.'*

"Twenty years on, Cohen is still specializing in typing with one hand, as proven by his Vanity

Fair *profile of Margot Robbie, in which he boldly decrees: 'She can be sexy and composed while naked, but only in character.' Well, it's hard to compose a sentence that makes sense when all your blood has rushed to the opposite end of your body from your brain. Robbie later described the piece, with admirable understatement, as really weird, and, while Cohen ends his article, appearing to be musing about having sex with her, Robbie says she walked away thinking, 'That was a really odd interview.' What was odd about it, Margot? He was just thinking about having sex with you. God, stuck up much?"*

I obviously don't endorse a ban on males interviewing female actors for magazines, but I do recommend they read Freeman's column before commencing.

ALARM BELLS SHOULD GO OFF

Some years ago, one of my students arranged an interview with a popular player on the Toronto Raptors. It was impressive that she managed to score the interview. But she was very inexperienced and her encounter didn't produce almost anything usable.

I found out after the fact that she had his number literally tattooed on her body. She wasn't really with him to do an interview; she was there to hang out with her crush.

I always say this: if you consider an interviewee to be drop-dead gorgeous, or if it's someone you idolize, warning bells should go off. Here's why. There's a good chance you'll shift your purpose from conducting a vigorous (and perhaps challenging) discussion to one in which your goal will be to make the person like you. If that happens, the chances of the interview succeeding diminish.

I remember listening to a Canadian national radio host interviewing a famous retired hockey player who had just written his autobiography. She gushed at the outset about how she was in a studio with one of her heroes; it went downhill from there, with sycophantic questions that were so hard to listen to that I turned the radio off. As 17th-century English poet, Anne Bradstreet, once said: "Sweet words are like honey. A little may refresh, but too much gluts the stomach."

Conversely, if you take an instant dislike to an interviewee, be equally careful. Unless you have empirical evidence to warrant your reaction, such as some abusive verbal behavior upon meeting the person, consider that your reaction might not be justified.

Sometimes, when we encounter someone who is similar to ourselves, we might not like that person, for psychological reasons that are not relevant to this book. Needless to say, a negative initial reaction might be an accurate reading of our Spidey senses, but it could also be a misread of someone who seems too much like some aspect of ourselves. As the cartoon character, Pogo, remarked, "We have met the enemy and he is us."

No matter the reason, when you have an immediate negative reaction to an interviewee, there's a strong chance you will be harder on that person, and it's less likely you'll believe what they say. That's preferable to sucking up to a hero, but it can be equally disastrous. The goal is to be open to whatever is presented to you, not to rush to judgment.

FLIRTING

Some interviews involve flirting, on both sides.

Most of it is harmless, the result of two people enjoying the heightened degree of verbal intimacy that can arise in some interviews. For the interviewee, it can be exciting to have so much attention focused on them, and to be listened to in a way they rarely experience. If the two parties hit it off, the exchange of questions and answers can be extremely enjoyable.

When the communication becomes mildly flirtatious it is likely harmless and lasts only for the duration of the interview.

But not always. Sometimes, one of the parties—often a male interviewee who is interviewed by a younger female—misinterprets the situation. He wants to take it further.

Some female students have made me aware of this when they've returned from an assignment and have complained about being hit on by "some random old guy." Fortunately, none of the instances ever amounted to more than a sad attempt to ask the student out.

Needless to say, no interviewer, female or male, has to put up with unwarranted verbal or physical abuse. In the past, the (likely male) journalism old-timers might have scoffed at a female reporter who returned from an interview upset at how she had been treated.

Hopefully, those days are in the past. Today, if the incident was concerning in any way, the interviewer should inform their superiors.

INTERVIEWING TRANSGENDER GUESTS

In April 2015, The Advocate, *an LGBTQ magazine, advised journalists not to focus on questions about genitalia when interviewing transgender people. The article criticized veteran journalist Katie Couric for having repeatedly done that when interviewing actor Laverne Cox and model-performer Carmen Carrera the year before.*

In response, Cox chided Couric: "The preoccupation with transition and surgery objectifies trans people, and then we don't get to really deal with the real lived experiences. The reality of trans people's lives is that so often we are targets of the community. Our unemployment rate is twice the national average. If you are a trans person of color, that rate is four times the national average. The homicide rate is highest among trans women. If we focus on transition, we don't actually get to talk about those things."

There are lots of online resources to guide you if you don't know how to conduct an interview with a transgender person. There's no excuse for ignorance or insensitivity.

MEAN TWEETS

It's not just actors and other famous women who get subjected to sexist comments (or much worse, as the #MeToo movement exposed). Many female journalists have to contend with it as well.

For an unpleasant taste of what that can be like, watch "Men Read Mean Tweets to Female Sports Reporters" on YouTube.

KEY TAKEAWAYS

- Be aware that some questions posed to a female can be sexist because they focus on matters that would not be asked of a male.
- If you find an interviewee extremely attractive or they are someone you consider a hero, be aware that you might want them to like you, resulting in tough questions not being asked.
- Before asking a trans person about their genitalia, be absolutely certain the question is absolutely relevant. It rarely, if ever, is.

EIGHTEEN: **INTERVIEWEE DEMANDS**

It's common for interviewees—or, often, their PR people—to demand a list of questions before an interview. I've been asked this many times. I'm not sure I could find a journalist who hasn't received such a request.

Should you comply? In general, the answer is no.

There are several reasons why:

- An interview is not a pre-planned exchange of questions and answers. If that were the case, organizations would hire a low-paid temp to conduct interviews from a printed list of agreed-to questions. An interview is an interaction between a skilled interviewer and the interviewee(s), with much of the valuable information coming out of follow-ups to answers.

- Many questions can't be predicted. They depend on what is said during the interview, or what pops into the interviewer's mind during the conversation.

- If an interviewee has a list of questions ahead of time, the chances are considerable the person will prepare safe, scripted answers, which is especially bad for a broadcast interview. It will sound like a PR piece, not a conversation. Many people prepare pat answers anyway (anticipating what will be asked), but if the person knows their responses could be broken down, explored, and challenged, the interview will have a much different feel.

THIS OFTEN WORKS

However, I'm happy to offer the PR person a sense of what areas or issues I want to explore; I find this almost always satisfies the requester.

There are always exceptions. Sometimes the only way to obtain a high-profile interview is to comply. However, I've found that most interviewees will answer questions that were not on the list sent to them.

My sense is that the request comes from two needs: one is control; the other is that many PR professionals think it demonstrates to their clients that they've done their job.

I WANT TO SEE THE ARTICLE OR HEAR THE BROADCAST BEFOREHAND

Mike McGowan, at the time an inexperienced writer, secured a plum assignment to profile feisty Pat Burns, then head coach of the Toronto Maple Leafs, for a November 1995 feature in *Toronto Life* magazine.

Early in a draft of his article, McGowan describes Burns running a Leafs practice, during which the volatile coach yells and swears at his players. The writer then recounts, in his article, what happened next:

"I'm sitting in the office, watching him read the beginning of this story [which McGowan had not yet finished or submitted to the magazine]. It was our second meeting, and before he would agree to answer any more questions, he wanted to see what I had written so far. A more experienced writer would have refused. I knew it was a mistake as soon as I made it. I had trespassed on journalistic practice."

Indeed he had. I never went to journalism school; developed my principles and practices on the run, often learning from experienced colleagues. One rule was drilled into me from day one: never share a draft or finished product with the person(s) quoted prior to broadcast or publication—especially if it contains anything the subject might not like.

When Burns had finished reading, he put down the article and turned to McGowan.

"You can't say that."

"What?"

"You can't write all those 'fucks.' You make me look like a fucking idiot." He starts counting. "You can't put five 'fucks' in."

"You said them [during a practice]."

Burns shook his head. "That's too many."

"People know you swear."

"But five? You can't do that. What about the kids in minor hockey?"

Obviously, the five "fucks," plus a few more, stayed in the story; and the exchange between the writer and the subject ended up being an engaging and illustrative anecdote. However, I wouldn't recommend letting an interviewee have a sneak peek.

There are rare occasions when it might be in your best interest to share part of your draft. Before noting when that might apply, let's look at the reasons why you shouldn't succumb to pressure (usually coming from a PR person) to provide an advance copy of your work:

It gives the people quoted in the article or broadcast a chance to lobby for anything they don't like to be changed or deleted. Worse, they could initiate legal action to accomplish the same result, in the form of an injunction to stop publication or broadcast.

Also, journalists have deadlines and can't be waiting for feedback or (*shudder*) sign-off from their interviewees.

WHAT DO YOU SAY WHEN ASKED TO SHARE A DRAFT?

What I tend to say is that it's not journalistic practice to show drafts beforehand; I then mention the issue of timing.

But, I add (if it's applicable), the story will be fact-checked. Someone will call and go over the quotes and details to ensure their accuracy. That was almost always the case when I mostly wrote magazine articles. I'm not sure it still happens to the same degree; I sense many outlets don't do this due to budget cuts.

I never use something I've heard some journalists say to counteract a request for a pre-publication review: "That's why we have libel laws. If you don't like what I wrote/broadcast/posted, you can sue me." That, to me, tells the person there could be material in the story they should be worried about.

WHEN MIGHT YOU SHARE?

It was George Plimpton, the famous American writer, editor, and sometime amateur athlete who first suggested to me that sending a draft to an interviewee could improve it. This was during my interview with him for *Asking Questions*. He was referring to the long interviews he and others did for *The Paris Review*, the exalted literary quarterly that he edited, along with some others, from its founding in 1953 until his death in 2003.

PM: Many journalists…feel there's a code that once an answer has been given, that's it.

GP: That's hopeless to me. That's ridiculous. It's the idea that the interviewer feels he has the goods and here it is down on tape and that's the truth, and why should he give it back to the guy who said it for a second chance. It's an unholy attitude, I think. And false. There are a hundred ways of saying the same sentence. The meaning is changed by inflection. Sometimes when you speak you get so carried away with yourself that you forget to make the salient points for your arguments.

For example, I just finished an interview with [writer and literary critic] Elizabeth Hardwick. She talks about the first lines in her books and I sent the thing back to her and said, "Elizabeth, can you add something here to make this just a bit more clear?" She was delighted to do so. I mean, who are we trying to fool? If you send the interview to someone, particularly the direct quotes, they will come back much better.

Plimpton was not the only person to have this kind of take on the subject. June Callwood, the prominent Canadian social justice journalist, surprised me in our interview for *Asking Questions:*

JC: I always read people their quotes. Always. When I write the piece, I phone them and tell them, "This is what I've got in quotes."

PM: Do they ever try and change them? Vet them to suit their purpose?

JC: Sometimes. They'll say, "I wish I hadn't put it that way." And if it's a reasonable change I usually go along with it. If it's something that could really hurt someone, I might say, "Well, let me tone it down," but I wouldn't take it out if it were necessary for the piece.

PM: What about quotes that really make someone look bad, in a critical story?

JC: I find if you read a bigot his quotes, for example, he usually says they sound fine, because that's the kind of' person he is. Reading people their quotes rarely causes any problems.

I don't read people their quotes (although fact checkers certainly have on my behalf, either verbatim or paraphrased). I have occasionally shared the wording of a quote on a complex topic (usually something technical because I'm so ungifted in this field) or, more typically, my *précis* of a technical matter. It might or might not have any quotes in it; but it is almost always a tight version of an issue or aspect that's not easy to understand.

Virtually every time I've done this, I've been sent an improved version of what I'd written. So, I would never say it's always a bad idea to engage with the interviewee during the editing process, but I urge caution.

AN EXPERT ON WHETHER JOURNALISTS SHOULD LET SOURCES LOOK OVER STORIES BEFORE PUBLICATION

In May 2020, Thomas Kent, a consultant on journalistic ethics and combating disinformation, who teaches at Columbia University, wrote the following (edited for length by me) in an article for the Poynter Institute:

"Journalists traditionally have a one-way relationship with sources. We take the information, publish the story and deal later with whatever the source thinks of what we wrote.

"This practice makes a lot of sense in investigative reporting when we interview powerful people for a story that may put them in a bad light. Giving them advance word of what we plan to write gives them opportunity to hide the evidence—or even get out ahead of us by denouncing our story before it's published.

"But the vast majority of our interviews are not adversarial. People we interview are often helping us out. Our relationship with them is a cooperative one. Our interviewees, being human, can overstate a case or leave out an important qualification.

"Some reporters have been known to send an entire story to a cooperative source before publication—not only to check the facts, but for a reality check on the whole thrust of the piece.

"Other than a quick call for an essential accuracy check, letting sources review content in any more detail is fraught with potential danger. Our right to quote material from sources as we heard it, in the fashion we want, is a precious one.

"In checking facts, we might also set clear expectations about what we're willing to do. When Tanya Mohn, a New York-based freelance journalist, feels a need to check a quote in a story, she tells the interviewee, 'I am unable to make changes or add anything unless something is factually incorrect.'"

KEY TAKEAWAYS

- Rarely provide a list of questions before an interview.
- Explain the reasons why you won't.
- Do offer, however, to send the areas/issues you will likely explore during the interview.

NINETEEN: **WHEN DIFFICULT CONDITIONS ARE IMPOSED**

In late 2005, Natasha Stoynoff, a writer for *People* magazine and a former student of mine, called me from New York City to discuss a dilemma she faced. (Transparency: She accused Donald Trump of assaulting her while on assignment at Mar-a-Lago, also in 2005, a claim I publicly verified more than 10 years later because she had told me about the incident immediately after it had happened.)

Stoynoff had been assigned to interview Pierce Brosnan in the restaurant of the St. Marks Hotel about his new movie, *The Matador*. Her editor also wanted her to ask him about the recent news that he was being replaced by Daniel Craig as James Bond in the upcoming *Casino Royale*. Brosnan's handlers, however, told her that any James Bond questions were off-limits.

What should I do? she asked me.

I began by cautioning her not to sneak in a Bond question during the conversation about *The Matador*, as that might close him up and make him feel blindsided, as some interviewers might do.

Rather, I suggested she engage in genuine conversation with him before the interview began, to establish rapport. Stoynoff is extremely personable and easy to like, as she's warm and enthusiastic. I then said, "Once you feel that has happened—and it needs to occur fairly quickly, as stars are on tight schedules—explain that you have a bit of a problem. Mention that it's something you hope the two of you can resolve."

The goal was to try to make it a mutual concern: tell him truthfully about being caught between what the editor wants and his people's restrictions. Ask: what advice did he have for her?

She followed my counsel and told me later that Brosnan, whom Stoynoff found to be "sweet and truly kind," listened and (I believe) appreciated her honesty. He agreed to allow questions about Bond as long as the focus of her article was about the film. Stoynoff assured him that was the case; from there, all went extremely well.

It's not unusual for conditions to be imposed on an interview, particularly when film stars are involved. In 1998, I was covering the Toronto International Film Festival when Christian Slater, one of the stars of the black comedy *Very Bad Things*, was brought to a round table to talk to about a half-dozen journalists, myself included. We'd been told ahead of time by a twitchy studio handler that no questions could be asked about Slater's recent incarceration for cocaine use.

However, his role in *Very Bad Things* required him to pretend to snort coke, which I figured was not an easy thing for a recent addict to contend with.

At one point, I brought this up and asked him if it had been difficult, as he was not long out of rehab. The handler went ballistic and started flapping her arms, reminding me that no questions about his drug use were permitted.

But Slater was nonplussed. "It's a fair question," he said, and provided an articulate and thoughtful answer; all the while, his handler glowered at me with homicidal fury.

My experience, over the years, has been that powerful,

successful people are usually willing to take on a tough question. Not always, but often enough for me to suggest the following tactic.

If something has been deemed off-limits beforehand, a condition which you've accepted, let the interviewee know about it when you think the timing is right (often towards the end of the interview).

Say something like this: "I was told that you're not comfortable talking about X and I just wanted to check in with you to see if that's the case. Or, if it's something you're okay to discuss."

Many powerful people don't like to be perceived as weak or frightened. Like Slater, if they know the question is relevant (and I understood from a relative who had beaten drug addiction that Slater having to snort pretend coke could trigger those old feelings), they want to address it.

It's not a violation of any undertaking to mention the agreement, at least not in my opinion. The one caveat is that if the person imposing the conditions is someone you'll need to work with again, you might be endangering that relationship by bringing it up.

OFF THE RECORD

There's a lot of confusion about this phrase.

What exactly does it mean? What do the following mean: "background," "deep background," and "not for attribution?" An August 2018 *New York Times* column about this topic conceded that, "There is no universally agreed-upon meaning for many of these terms—and *The Times* has no precise descriptions in its own internal guidelines—making it difficult to sketch out even working definitions."

The *Times* writer, Matt Flegenheimer, suggested that "A reporter's best course of action is to establish jargon-free parameters in plain English at the start: Can a source be quoted by name? Can we use the information if we leave out the name? Can we at least describe the source's job?"

If you're working on an investigation, you should discuss this issue before interviewing a source. I've found that some interviewees confuse "off the record" with "not for attribution" (the source is not identified). If you're proposing the latter, it can be helpful to explain that if they tell you something, you won't say where the information came from.

If that's what you end up doing, there's a caveat: make sure the source can't be identified in some other way. I learned this the hard way.

Early in my career, I worked on a lengthy article about the use of PEDs (performance-enhancing drugs) in the Canadian Olympic community. One of my most helpful sources was a member of the women's track-and-field team, who told me her coach was pressuring her to take steroids. "My husband and I talked it over," she said, "and we were concerned that the drugs might affect my ability to become pregnant later on, so I decided not to take them."

I reported this anecdote and, of course, protected her identity. There were a large number of female members on the track-and-field team so I was confident my source would be anonymous. Unfortunately, it didn't cross my mind to ask how many female members of the team were married. Turns out the answer was two: my source, whom I had described as an up-and-comer, and one other, who was one of Canada's most accomplished international stars.

The woman telephoned me the day after my story ran to say her coach had gone ballistic when he read it. I was devastated at my ignorant betrayal; she was gracious, saying she felt her career wasn't going anywhere and maybe it was time to retire and focus on having that baby she had talked about.

THE POST-COMMENT CONDITION

A common occurrence is perhaps the trickiest for interviewers to manage: after a source tells you something juicy, they say, "But that's off the record, of course." What to do?

Some reporters, especially if they work for a newspaper, will say sorry, you told me and I'm going to use it. Others might be willing to take a moment and discuss how to deal with this situation.

Baseball reporter Shi Davidi says, "This has happened to me many times. Generally, I try to respect their concerns. If you're on the beat, you can't think in terms of a single story. You have to play a long game. Do you want to burn somebody for one story or do you want to create a relationship that's going to feed you over the long term? If people think you're just going to take what they say and run with it [no matter what], that you're going to screw them, you have no chance whatsoever of having a long-term relationship with them. If I want somebody's trust, I'm going to have to give that back to them."

I remember being given a damning quote by a mid-level Ontario bureaucrat. It was for a story about a nasty fight among various groups over who owned access to a waterfront beach in cottage country. He told me something he shouldn't have about the government's position, then immediately realized his mistake. To his credit, he said, "Well, I did say it, so I guess you can use it."

"What will happen to you if I do?" I asked.

"I'll probably get fired."

It was a great quote but, as I discussed afterwards with my editor, was it worth the man's job? We both decided it wasn't and didn't use it. I believe we did the right thing.

For another magazine story, someone I thought was a bit sleazy badmouthed my main character and then played the "off-the-record" card. I printed what he had said and he was furious. But this man was interviewed all the time—I'm guessing he'd done hundreds of interviews over many decades, with journalists from around the world—and knew exactly what he was doing. He tried to play me, and I didn't like it. So, to me, whether to agree to a post-comment embargo is a case-by-case decision.

My best advice is to have your own ethical guidelines about "off the record." Is it a black-and-white issue for you (most media trainers tell their clients there is no such thing as "off the record"; they advise their clients not to say anything they don't want used) or are you willing to discuss how to respond when it arises? I'm obviously in the latter group, but I tend to work on long-term projects, so I have the luxury of time. That is not available to reporters with daily declines.

KEY TAKEAWAYS

- Know what "off-the-record" means and be able to explain it to an interviewee.
- Understand that some interviewees confuse "off-the-record" with "not for attribution."
- If you disguise a source, make sure their identity can't easily be determined.

TWENTY: **COMFORT THE AFFLICTED/ AFFLICT THE COMFORTABLE**

I once interviewed a property owner for CBC Radio because of public criticism that some local landlords had been "absentee" or "unwilling to make repairs." Even though I was a renter at the time, I had sympathy for landlords, as I knew some tenants sometimes refused to pay rent, trashed the place they occupied, and were generally difficult. I also thought the "absentee" epithet was ridiculous. Did renters expect every owner of a building to live on the premises?

Despite my personal feelings, I conducted the interview in a challenging manner. That meant presenting the allegations that had been leveled. Instead of calmly explaining his perspective, the man attacked me for even mentioning them. He was defensive and belligerent and came across in what I had to believe was the exact opposite way in which he had hoped to be perceived. He seemed to take any questions that weren't softball in nature as a personal attack.

This reinforced the perception that some (if not many) landlords were harsh towards, and uncaring about, their tenants. I recall thinking he hadn't represented himself very well.

He stormed out of the studio before I could explain that my job was to represent the underdog, the weakest and least powerful party in a dispute.

HOLD THEIR FEET TO THE FIRE

I had been taught, almost from my first day on the job, that journalists were supposed to "comfort the afflicted and afflict the comfortable."

The quote's origins are a bit muddy, but its message is at the heart of what we do.

The first part—comfort the afflicted—means we help give a voice to those who might not have one. A large corporation or government department, for example, has a slew of well-paid professionals whose job is to represent the interests of the people and the place where they work. They tend to have considerable resources available to help them do just that. A single mother fighting an unfair eviction notice, as one example, doesn't have that advantage.

Afflict the comfortable means holding the feet of those in power to the fire. As a result, governments tend to perceive the media as the enemy; but if journalists are doing their jobs properly, they're just trying to hold a government, corporation, or individual accountable for their actions.

Some journalists, of course, take this quasi-opposition role to an extreme and attack the government or a powerful corporate body in a way that seems personal or as a kind of sport.

But the vast majority, I believe, see their role the same way Pulitzer Prize-winning journalist Glenn Greenwald does: "A key purpose of journalism is to provide an adversarial check on those who wield the greatest power, by shining a light on what they do in the dark, and informing the public about those acts."

Adversarial, however, isn't a synonym for "attack." It means that you try to make interviewees explain themselves, even if you agree with them, as I did with the landlord.

I've tried to convince my non-media friends that a tough, adversarial question is actually what they should hope for, although without much success.

"If you can provide a convincing response, especially for a broadcast interview, it serves you well with the audience," I'd tell them. "And for print, it can accomplish the same with the reporter."

Being served a softball question can actually backfire. "It might seem like an easy one for you to deal with, but if an audience thinks you've not been challenged, how does that benefit you in the long run?"

My experience is that adversarial questions tend to produce better answers. They can also help you assess an interviewee's position on a topic. If the person can't be convincing when answering challenging questions or explaining a policy/position, it's noteworthy. I wouldn't assume the person is being untruthful or evasive—there could be other reasons for a poor response—but it certainly suggests something isn't right.

Some of my students have wondered whether it's rude or mean to put an interviewee on the spot. I leave it to Helen Thomas, who covered the White House as a reporter during the administrations of 10 U.S. presidents, to supply a succinct response: "I don't think a tough question is disrespectful."

WE DON'T DO PR

Writer George Orwell once reputedly said, "Journalism is printing what someone else does not want published; everything else is public relations."

I sense that a lot of what appears in print or on electronic platforms today likely falls into the "everything else" category, although I think some of those stories can serve a valuable function.

No matter what you're interviewing people about, it's important to remember you're not their PR agent, although some interviewees and, more commonly, some of their handlers, think that's your role. Your job is to ask the right questions, whether the interviewee likes them or not.

Some interviewers have asked me whether I agree it's best to save the toughest questions until the end, so they can make a fast getaway if the person verbally attacks them.

I don't subscribe to this form of cowardice.

You should ask a question at the most appropriate time. That could mean dealing with it at the outset, leading up to it in the middle of the interview, or leaving it until near the end—whichever best meets your goals.

WALTER CRONKITE'S LIBERAL TAKE

"I think being a liberal, in the true sense, is being nondoctrinaire, nondogmatic, non-committed to a cause—but examining each case on its merits. Being left of center is another thing; it's a political position.

"I think most [journalists] by definition have to be

liberal; if they're not liberal, by my definition of it, then they can hardly be good [journalists]. If they're preordained dogmatists for a cause, then they can't be very good journalists; that is, if they carry it into their journalism," Walter Cronkite, *the* CBS Evening News *giant, said in a 1973 interview in* Playboy.

NOAM CHOMSKY ON BEING EMBEDDED

Britannica *defines embedding as "the practice of placing journalists within and under the control of one side's military during an armed conflict." It came into prominence during the Iraq War in 2003.*

"No honest journalist should be willing to describe himself or herself as 'embedded,'" the noted linguist and social/media critic, Noam Chomsky, said in his book, Imperial Ambitions: Conversations on the Post-9/11 World. *"To say, 'I'm an embedded journalist' is to say, 'I'm a government propagandist.'"*

OBJECTIVITY

I've never believed in objectivity; I don't see how it can possibly be attained. No matter how hard we might try, we bring an entire lifetime of experience and influences to each interview and story we do. As the 20th-century Austrian-American scientist Heinz von Foerster said: "Objectivity is the delusion that observations could be made without an observer."

Henry Luce, the prolific publisher of magazines such as *Time, Fortune,* and *Sports Illustrated,* echoed that sentiment: "Show me a man who claims he is objective and I'll show you a man with illusions."

Are the questions you ask (or don't ask) objectively chosen? I don't believe so. Yes, the story might demand that you pose them. But how you do so, and at what point in an interview, are subjective decisions. Likewise, when you write or produce a piece: What do you lead with? Who gets quoted? Where and for how long?

Rather than objectivity, I recommend you aim for fairness, accuracy, and balance (if applicable; some stories, like the Holocaust or slavery, just don't lend themselves to balance).

IT DOESN'T HAVE TO BE SWEET, CAROLINE

"I don't trust an interview that's 100 percent positive. It's not grounded," singer Neil Diamond *told* The Globe and Mail *in November 2005. "Saying that this is a wonderful album, he's great, the songs are great, that doesn't do it for me unless you're talking about* Sgt. Pepper.*"*

KEY TAKEAWAYS

- Our primary role is to give a voice to those who are not in power.
- Most interviews are "adversarial" in nature: we challenge interviewees to explain themselves.
- There is no such thing as true objectivity.

TWENTY-ONE: **BRAIN-BASED INTERVIEWING**

In 2003, I interviewed Frank Byrnes, a former intelligence officer who had worked with the Toronto and Montreal police forces, the RCMP, and CSIS (Canadian Security Intelligence Service) before becoming a consultant based in Ottawa. A specialist in interviewing skills, Byrnes was trained in neurolinguistic programming and brain-compatible learning. He's the founder and president of Human Potential Consultants Inc.

Although this conversation, which originally appeared in *Report on Fraud*, a publication I wrote and edited for the Canadian Institute of Chartered Accountants on behalf of my forensic accounting clients, focuses on Byrnes' law enforcement experience, I think much of it also pertains to journalism and other forms of interviewing.

The following is an edited version of what appeared in *ROF*.

PM: Did you receive interview training as a police officer?

FB: Only once, when I was with the Montreal city police. A lieutenant detective told me to put my foot on a subject's testicles and, if I thought he was telling the truth, keep the pressure light. But if I thought he was starting to snow me, lean a little harder.

PM: This is not what you recommend, I assume.

FB: Definitely not (*laughs*). I take the opposite approach.

To be consistently successful, I believe an interviewer has to understand how the mind works, how the brain is wired, and how to use that information to develop trust and rapport with an interviewee. Once you achieve that, you have a very high chance of obtaining the information you're looking for.

PM: This is the brain-based interviewing that you now teach.

FB: That's right. A pioneer in this field, Avinoam Sapir, who's a former Israeli polygraph officer, says, "Everyone wants to tell everything to everyone." I observed this when I was a police officer. If a suspect was roughed up, he might talk but he'd only tell enough to get the rough stuff to stop. I learned early on that by connecting and communicating with suspects in an empathetic way, they'd tell me a lot more.

PM: How would you define brain-based interviewing?

FB: In simple terms, the brain is wired to always respond in certain ways under certain conditions. For example, the vast majority of people—about 85 percent—always look up to their right when creating or fabricating an image. Also, therefore, when they're lying. You also need to know that the eyes move to different places when they're remembering an image and when they're creating one.

PM: But 15 percent don't. How do you reconcile that?

FB: You ask them a series of neutral, non-threatening questions, like they do in a polygraph test, to see where their eyes go when they're telling the truth.

PM: So brain-based interviewing is really about reading people?

FB: Absolutely, including yourself. An interviewer has to know what he or she does that can hinder or help the interview to work. One of the biggest mistakes interviewers make is to go too fast. They want to rush to the result. But in doing so, they make it harder to achieve those results. We suggest they slow down and follow a series of six speed bumps, as we call them.

PM: I understand the first one is "state and self-fulfilling prophecies."

FB: State refers to the interviewer's emotional state going into an interview. If you're calm and open and have a positive expectation, then no problem. But if you're tense and your body language is negative and hostile, the interviewee is going to sense that and likely won't trust you or open up. You need to calm down, relax, whatever it takes, to get into a more resourceful state.

PM: Where do self-fulfilling prophecies come into play?

FB: Study after study has proven that if you believe something is going to happen—for example, that the person is going to lie—then that's what you will find. One example was an experiment done some years ago in New York City. A group of teachers were told they had been selected, because of their superior teaching skills, to work with a class of gifted students chosen from across the city. At the end of the year, the students had achieved impressive results, far above the norm. But the students had not been gifted. They'd been chosen randomly. When the teachers were told this—that their expectations had influenced the outcome—they said, but wait, we're all gifted teachers. That's when the researchers told them that they too had been randomly chosen.

PM: The second speedbump is "rapport and trust."

FB: One of the keys in establishing rapport and trust is to match and mirror a person's posture, language, mood, etc. For example, if the interviewee is sitting with her hands folded across her chest defensively, you do the same. But as the interview progresses, you unfold yours and adopt an open posture. She'll [likely] do the same. Likewise for speech. Say the person is speaking in a loud, angry voice. You can't establish rapport if you counter with a calm, monotone voice. Instead, start out loud and edgy, then begin to lower the volume, soften the tone. The other person will then do the same. By doing this you can lead them into a state where they are more calm, open, willing to communicate.

PM: The next is "active listening."

FB: Listening, as I think we all know, is one of our weakest skills. I like to say that we need to listen with our eyes and intuition and heart as well as our ears. Most of how we communicate truthfully is through our body and our voice. What we say can be untruthful, but the body never lies.

PM: The fourth is "reading people."

FB: People are primarily visual, auditory, or kinesthetic speakers. Visual speakers use words like see and visualize, etc. They speak quickly and use lots of hand movements. Auditory speakers talk about hearing something, saying something, or, that doesn't ring a bell, and speak slower than visual types. Kinesthetic people say things like, I didn't grasp what you're getting at, this is heavy, take me by the hand and walk me through it. They speak the slowest of the three groups.

PM: So the interviewer should use the same language and speed?

FB: Yes. [By the way] just before [interviewees] are about to tell you something important, [they] often look down...and tilt to the left [or] right.

PM: Next speed bump: "framing the message."

FB: We tend to frame things based on our needs: "I need you to tell me" [for example]. What works much better is to frame questions based on what is important for the interviewee.

PM: The sixth bump is "assertiveness." What does that mean in this context?

FB: One thing it means is to be direct. One of my colleagues used to be a polygraph operator and profiler with the Quebec Provincial Police. He says that he often obtained confessions before even having to administer the polygraph. Know how he did it? He simply asked: "Did you do it?" Previous interrogators had skirted around the question, used all kinds of tricks to get them to confess, but had never just plain asked.

PM: What do you say to people who think this is all psychobabble?

FB: Experience is the best teacher. Try it out. If it works for you, keep doing it. If it doesn't, then try something else.

KEY TAKEAWAYS

- Study after study has proven that if you believe something is going to happen—for example, that the person is going to lie—then that's what you will find.
- One of the biggest mistakes interviewers make is to go too fast.
- People are primarily visual, auditory, or kinesthetic speakers. If you recognize one of these dominant traits in a person, it could influence how you word questions.

TWENTY-TWO: **TRUST AND RAPPORT**

Seven seconds. Maybe not even that long.

That's the amount of time you have to make an impression on a person, *Forbes* magazine reported in a June 2018 article.

"Within the first seven seconds of meeting, people will have a solid impression of who you are—and some research suggests a tenth of a second is all it takes to start determining traits like trustworthiness," wrote Serenity Gibbons, a former editor at *The Wall Street Journal*.

These numbers are readily quoted in numerous articles, but I have no idea whether they're accurate. What I do know, from years of conducting interviews, is that your initial contact in person, on a video link, or on the phone, can affect the outcome of the interview.

A rocky start can be overcome, but not always. Initial mistrust, on the interviewee's part, can be mitigated if an interviewer asks reasonable questions in a reasonable manner. But why start off on the wrong foot? From the moment you say hello to an interviewee, how you comport yourself is critical to conducting an effective interview.

In fact, it's smart to behave at the highest professional level from the moment you enter a building, or any other interview location. For example, be mindful of what you say or do when riding an elevator to a person's office. The person standing next to you could be the interviewee's colleague.

Treat a receptionist, secretary, or any other support worker the way you would the interviewee. Be aware, especially in these days of omnipresent security cameras, that unseen eyes might be on you, as you wait for the interviewee in a boardroom, lobby, or videoconference waiting room. Don't get on your phone and discuss anything related to the story you're working on. Looking around is normal but avoid doing anything that would make you feel guilty if someone caught you.

TRUST

Establishing trust is critical. If the person believes you're sincere and straightforward, the potential for successful communication increases dramatically.

Trust is gained partly through nonverbal behavior. Are you friendly without being phony? Do you establish eye contact? Do you display non-defensive body language? Are you smiling?

The importance of a smile can't be underestimated. A 1978 University of Miami study found that over 43 percent of the attention we focus on someone is devoted to their eyes. "Smiles are an integral part of human and primate communications, and they usually convey a positive message. Genuine smiles (the ones that involve the muscles surrounding the eyes) induce positive feelings among those who are smiled at," a 2015 article in *Psychology Today* said.

The magazine calls eye contact "the strongest form of nonverbal communication."

Former President Bill Clinton was renowned for his intense eye contact. During a 2008 interview with

David Letterman, actress Gillian Anderson (best known for her role as Special Agent Scully on *The X-Files* and Prime Minister Margaret Thatcher in *The Crown*) shared her belief that the secret behind Clinton's sex appeal was lingering eye contact. "We all, mostly women, line up. And when he gets to you, he takes your hand and makes eye contact. After he leaves and he moves on to the next person, he looks back at you and seals the deal," she said.

Do you look at the person you're interviewing? How would you describe your gaze? I fix my eyes on the interviewee, but not in a way that might make them uncomfortable.

Trust is also gained by how you express yourself. Do you present yourself as trustworthy, honest, and professional? Or do you avoid eye contact, mumble, and act evasively when asked basic questions about the upcoming interview?

If it's the latter, the interviewee may become overly cautious and reticent, which is not what you want.

RAPPORT

Rapport can be established by finding areas of common interest to discuss prior to the interview starting. It might be by talking about the news, weather and sports, the mention of a mutual acquaintance, or by discussing a topic in which you both share an interest.

Perhaps you and the interviewee have something similar in your backgrounds. For example, in early 1980, I interviewed retired federal Conservative leader Robert Stanfield for a radio documentary on the tenth anniversary of the imposition of the War Measures Act in Canada. That was when then-Prime Minister Pierre Elliott Trudeau suspended civil liberties in Canada during an apparent insurrection by Quebec radicals.

I only needed a few comments, but I didn't sit down, pull out my tape recorder and say, "Mr. Stanfield, October 1970, your thoughts."

First of all, he didn't know me. Secondly, he was in his mid-60s. I had no idea how vibrant his memory would be about his time in parliamentary opposition when Liberal leader Trudeau invoked the controversial Act.

Instead, I began by talking about how my Scottish father had learned some Gaelic, a language still spoken in parts of Nova Scotia. (Stanfield was a former premier of the province.) Our brief conversation on that topic, and on my life in Scotland until leaving with my parents at age seven, allowed us to get to know each other a bit before getting down to the actual interview.

Once I felt he trusted me, I took out my tape recorder. But I still didn't jump right into his recollections of October 1970. Instead, I slowly walked him through what he remembered of the political landscape in Quebec during the 1950s and '60s. By the time we got to 1970, his memory was in full bloom.

Sometimes, there's no time to establish trust and rapport. I once had a telephone interview lined up with former NHL star Steve Yzerman about a topic he cared about deeply—eye protection while playing hockey and other sports. It turned out, however, that the day of our scheduled interview was the day Yzerman, the team's executive director, would be announcing which players had made the roster for Canada's hockey team in the 2010 Winter Olympics in Vancouver.

Ever gracious, he didn't cancel the interview, which he asked to be held at 6:45 a.m. Toronto time because of his intense schedule that day. He told my editor he would call me, which he did, exactly as promised.

Some friends who shared my love of hockey knew I'd be talking to Yzerman. They urged me to try to pry advance information out of him about the Olympic team.

I did no such thing, as I knew he would never leak anything. And it would waste some of the time I'd been given with him.

Instead, the first moments in our conversation went something like this:

PM: How much time do you have?

SY: Fifteen minutes. I have another call at seven.

PM: That's a real 15 minutes.

SY: Yes.

PM: Normally I'd engage in some warmup conversation before getting down to business. Are you okay if I don't do that? And that I ask my important questions first, even if they might seem all over the place.

SY: Absolutely. Let's go.

I then began to pick out the questions I had to have answered. He gave great responses. And at 7:00 he said goodbye.

While developing trust and rapport is important, it's not always the right approach. Some times, especially if you're attacked for being a journalist, you have to fight back. You need to read each situation and decide what will work best in any given circumstance.

KEY TAKEAWAYS

- Develop trust by acting in an open, honest, and trustworthy manner.
- Develop rapport by finding something(s) of common interest/connection prior to the formal interview beginning.
- Eye contact is the strongest form of nonverbal communication.

TWENTY-THREE: **LISTENING**

I call them the Holy Trinity of interviewing: listening, silence, and tone.

When I started out, I thought an interviewer's most important skill was the ability to formulate brilliant questions.

How wrong I was.

Asking insightful questions is, of course, essential, but it's not at the top of my list; far from it, actually.

Much of what transpires during an interview involves one or more members of my so-called Trinity. Listening helps lead to the next question. Silence gives the interviewee time to delve further into an answer. And tone allows you to pose difficult or sensitive questions in a way that increases the chances of having them answered.

LISTEN UP

There are countless articles online that explore why so many of us have poor listening skills and offer tips on how to improve them. My goal isn't to add to that list. Rather, I'll offer a few observations about why listening is so important for interviewers, and why it's often a weakness.

"If I could write only one chapter about interviewing, it would be about listening," I wrote in *Asking Questions*.

"And if I could write only one sentence, it would be this: the more deeply you listen, the more eloquently people will speak."

Imagine what it would be like to talk to an audience of people who are all on their phones. Or sharing your innermost thoughts with someone who is checking out other people as you speak.

We need to know the other person is listening when we communicate something important with them. As American psychiatrist and author M. Scott Peck wrote in *The Road Less Traveled*, "You cannot truly listen to anyone and do something else at the same time."

A SKILL TO WORK ON

"You're not listening!" is a frequent human complaint.

A 2019 *Psychology Today* article focused on the importance of listening attentively in personal relationships. "Recent studies," the magazine noted, linked attentive listening to "higher relationship satisfaction in couples."

And yet, it added, "We are all, to varying degrees, failing at this simple task. Perhaps in today's technological age, we are more used to dividing our attention than ever before. Many of us are rarely fully present. We may notice that no matter what's going on in conversation, a beep from our phone somehow takes priority. A good question to ask ourselves is how often do we find ourselves saying, 'Wait just a sec, I'm getting a call,' or, 'Sorry, I just have to respond to a text?'"

It takes considerable effort to listen steadily for 20 minutes, an hour, or even longer during an interview. I find two hours close to my maximum interview limit.

Listening intently for that amount of time can be exhausting, as journalist Roy MacGregor describes:

"I can go out and interview someone for an hour and that person will have the sense of being with someone who is uncommonly comfortable," he said. "They're confronted by someone who is sitting there in a completely relaxed state of mind, who seems on the verge of falling asleep. But I go out of the interview completely exhausted. Inside, I'm churning so fast, it's as if I'm playing 19 games of squash. And yet my body gives off a sense of total relaxation. I don't know how, because I'm not relaxed. I'm trying to remember things, remember what I have to return to. And I am trying to act like it is just a casual conversation and much of it doesn't matter, even though all of it matters."

AVOID DISTRACTIONS

For interviews that are not in-person, your phone and computer can be tempting distractions. If you want to improve your listening skills, turn them off before the interview begins, unless you need to access them during the conversation.

If you must leave them on, develop the discipline to use only when necessary.

Your phone can also be an especial distraction during an in-person or Zoom interview. An interviewee could perceive your quick glance to see what just came in as rude and unprofessional.

OUR JOB IS TO REVEAL

If the interviewee says something you think is implausible or even outrageous, do you keep listening? Or do you try to prove them wrong?

Our obligation is not to proselytize but to listen to, and perhaps reveal, what the interviewee thinks. Former CBC journalist Ralph Benmergui, author of *I Thought He Was Dead: A Spiritual Memoir*, once put it well to me: "I'm not there to express what I think. My responsibility is to listen to what the person says. If the person is a homophobe, I don't need to say that I'm not. What I want to do is understand and expose why the person feels that way. That's my job."

Despite how exhausting it is to give someone your undivided attention for an extended period of time, don't depend on your equipment to listen for you. When taping a conversation, especially over the phone, it can be easy to tune out.

I once did a phone interview on a hot afternoon for a book I was writing, while I was exhausted and helping care for our new baby. It was with a university professor who was an expert on aging. She was extremely helpful but spoke to me as if she was defending a PhD dissertation.

Although she made many valuable points, a lot of what she said was long-winded, hard for me to follow, and of no obvious use for the book. I have a vivid memory of wanting to let her drone on, then listen to the tape later.

But I didn't. It was a good thing I fought the urge to tune out because, at the end of our lengthy chat, she said, "I just want to make sure I've communicated clearly, so if you don't mind, can you summarize what you've understood from our conversation?"

I was able to do so and felt great relief at how close I came to what could have been a most embarrassing moment.

I've only been asked this question on one other occasion—by another academic, interestingly. Both times, I was able to recap what was said. Otherwise, these may have entered the annals of my most embarrassing missteps.

WE ALL MISS SOMETHING

"I learned from listening to taped interviews that sometimes I wasn't listening intently enough. I'd go over a tape and wonder how I missed that," sports journalist Shi Davidi says.

When transcribing tapes, assess how well you listened. If you drifted off at times, try to determine why, and resolve not to do it next time.

WHAT TO LISTEN FOR

What people say.
What they don't say.
How they do both.
The second point is worth another beat. Management consultant and author Peter Drucker believes, "The most important thing in communication is hearing what isn't said."

WHY WE DON'T LISTEN

In 2019, *Fast Company* magazine offered some reasons why so many of us are bad listeners. What follows is advice from Fred Halstead, author of *Leadership Skills That Inspire Incredible Results*, with some of my personal observations added to the mix:

- Our natural desire is to talk. Most of us want to create a favorable image, and one way to appear knowledgeable and smart is by sharing what we know. This can stop us from listening to the other person because we're thinking of what our response will be.

- As the journalist and storyteller Stuart McLean once said, "Basically, listening for most of us is waiting for a chance to start talking again." Stephen Covey, who wrote *The 7 Habits of Highly Effective People,* echoed that sentiment. "Most people do not listen with the intent to understand," he said. "They listen with the intent to reply."

- We're judging others. When someone says something we think is wrong or misguided, it's easy to dismiss their input. Rather than judging, hear them out. Maybe we're missing something.

- Ego gets in the way. It tells you, "I'm really smart. How much do I need to listen to this person?" Halstead says. "It prevents you from listening to people you think are intellectually or socially inferior."

- Distraction is one of the greatest impediments to listening well.

- We're exhausted. It's more difficult to be an active listener when we're tired.

YOU EASILY CAN MISS THINGS

On a more mundane level, there are risks to simply keeping the conversation moving, with no regard for what is really being said or taking place. The danger is that you'll miss out on the best information and, in the process, possibly make a fool of yourself.

This clearly was demonstrated in a broadcast observed by the globetrotting interviewer David Frost: "I remember watching a show in England once: [The actor] George Raft was on, and so was a woman, a sort of revue star. Now George Raft is a celebrity, and it was his first visit to England, so he was quite a catch. He sat there and said, 'There was one time when I was in trouble with the Internal Revenue Department. They said if I didn't pay my back taxes, I might go to jail. Then I got a phone call from Frank Sinatra and Frank said, 'I couldn't bear it if my childhood hero, George Raft, was in trouble. So I'm sending over a check for, let's say, a million dollars. If you can pay it back, do; if not, it doesn't matter.'

"Now, this is a fascinating story, and there are a million things one could ask. But the host turned to the [revue star] and said, 'Tell me, have *you* ever had problems with money?' And she said something like, 'Well, I once lost two shillings in the sweepstakes.' Well, you just wanted to hurl something, you were so desperate to hear the rest of the Raft-Sinatra story."

If you're not a strong listener, make it a mission to work on improving this vital skill. Whenever you drift off, recognize it's happening and will yourself to keep listening.

LISTEN TO HEMINGWAY

One of our primary jobs as interviewers is to listen to people at a level they rarely experience.

As Ernest Hemingway wrote in a 1949 letter of advice to a young writer: "When people talk, listen completely. Most people never listen."

KEY TAKEAWAYS

- Listening well is one of our weakest skills.
- You cannot truly listen to anyone and do something else at the same time.
- One of your most important responsibilities is to hear what isn't said.

TWENTY-FOUR: **SILENCE**

I really came to understand the power of silence in the early 1980s, during a performance of the play, *The Jail Diary of Albie Sachs*. Canadian actor R. H. Thomson played the title role, the powerful story of a white South African lawyer who was imprisoned in the early 1960s for opposing apartheid.

Just before the end of Act One, Sachs addressed the audience directly from the set of his jail cell. He wanted to give us a sense of what it was like to endure his 168 days of solitary confinement. "I'm going to make you sit and stare. You mustn't talk or read your programs, look at other people. For two minutes, you must sit and stare." And with that, as the stage directions decree, "He goes to his bunk and lies down."

The production I attended was in a small venue, and the audience was close to the stage. No one, I sensed, felt they could violate the sanctity of the moment by coughing, fidgeting or, God forbid, speaking. By the end of the two minutes, which lasted an uncomfortably long time, the room thundered with a profound silence, if I may be forgiven the cliché.

Silence is not the absence of sound, as so many seem to believe. BBC interviewer and filmmaker, Louis Theroux, gives it this poetic description: "Silence is like a hole; it's meaningless without the earth around it."

Often, silence is indeed full of meaning. Interviewers who understand this use it effectively. Those who fear it lose valuable opportunities to elicit possible gems from their interviewees.

In his 2012 book, *The Power of Silence: The Riches That Lie Within*, UK journalist Graham Turner notes that, "For many people in the West, the very idea of silence is strange and unattractive, if not actually forbidding."

He illustrates how our language reflects this: "We talk about an uncomfortable silence, an awkward silence, an embarrassing silence, an oppressive silence, a stony silence, an ominous silence, a silence you can cut with a knife, a deathly silence."

Addressing the culture of the time (he published his book at least ten years prior to me writing this one, an eternity when it comes to issues such as reduced attention span and the effects of social media on our need for constantly changing content), Turner describes silence as "counter-cultural."

Silence, he adds, is widely regarded as "nothing more than a disagreeable hole that must be filled at all costs, and by whatever means comes to hand."

As UK psychotherapist Hymie Wise has said, "Silence is the most important thing in psychotherapy. In every session with a patient, whether it's with an individual or a couple, silence is the background to everything. All that is said comes from silence and returns to silence. Once you are aware of that fact, you realize that silence is a presence."

HOW SILENCE HELPS AN INTERVIEWER

Silence is particularly important in two types of interviews. The first is when a person is on message track. The second is when they're trying to remember something emotional, deeply personal, or difficult to speak about.

Message track is where a spokesperson—perhaps a politician or corporate executive—has been coached to repeat a prepared answer to an unwelcomed question.

One way to combat this is to confront it. The former Toronto morning-radio host, Andy Barrie, who often had only a few minutes for each on-air interview, sometimes prefaced a follow-up question with this: "Without reverting to message track, could you tell us..." That sometimes worked.

Another strategy is to say nothing. It's been observed that most people, when confronted with silence, feel compelled to talk. Do try this at home, by the way.

This is how it often transpires: The interviewer asks a question. The guest responds. The interviewer then says nothing, smiles, and gently nods in the interviewee's direction. Faced with the discomfort of the silence, the person, usually after a brief pause, continues to answer.

Many people practice what I call a prepared tier-one answer to a question. We do this when prepping for a job interview, when explaining why we did something wrong, or when asking for a favor or other benefit.

Some interviewees do it in anticipation of a challenging question.

But if no follow-up question is posed after the interviewee offers a prepared response, many become less articulate, less confident in what they say. Often, but by no means always, what they say next is more revealing, more helpful to the interviewer.

Chip Scanlan, a writer at the Poynter Institute, puts it more directly. "Shut your mouth. Wait. People hate silence and rush to fill it," he says. "Ask your question. Let them talk. If you have to, count to ten. Make eye contact, smile, nod, but don't speak. You'll be amazed at the riches that follow."

One of my favorite anecdotes involved the Canadian broadcaster Pierre Pascau. He once told a journalism conference about an interview he'd done with Jean Drapeau, the flamboyant and controversial mayor of Montreal.

"He's a very funny character," Pascau began. "All kinds of people from the CBC had interviewed him and attacked him because they hated his guts. They wanted to embarrass Drapeau and make him look like a fool, and they asked him all kinds of very tough questions. But they made fools of themselves because Drapeau doesn't say what he doesn't want to say."

Pascau's interview took place during a municipal election. "He called and asked to be on my show. I didn't want him...but I said come anyway. I introduced him and I said, 'This is the Mayor of Montreal, Mr. Jean Drapeau. Okay, Mr. Drapeau, what do you have to say?' And he started talking and he went on [for a while] and I looked at him with a polite smile on my face and I said nothing.

"And then he said, 'Mr. Pascau, you are making faces at me.' And I said, 'No, Mr. Drapeau, I'm not making faces.' 'Yes, you are making faces! I can see you making them!' 'No, I'm not making...' 'YES, YOU ARE MAKING FACES!' And I said, 'Who would dare make faces at the mayor of Montreal?' And so he flew into a rage, a tantrum and made a scene, like a spoiled brat, and it was beautiful. You know, it's the nicest interview I ever had with the mayor of Montreal and I said nothing. I just smiled."

Eric Malling, perhaps Canada's most feared interviewer when he was co-host of the CBC program *the fifth estate* and CTV's *W5*, said, "I earn my money talking to people before the camera rolls and I make my money keeping my mouth shut after it starts to roll.

"The most important thing about interviewing is knowing when to keep quiet. People hate silence. If somebody answers a question and you can tell they're not quite finished, say nothing and they'll start again. And often what comes out is the real answer."

As Debussy said, "the music is not in the notes but in the silence between."

ALLOW TIME TO RECALL

Silence is also extremely useful when exploring a topic that might affect an interviewee's strong emotions. If you were asked to recall a traumatic or deeply emotional experience in your life, ask yourself whether you can or would disgorge it all immediately, in perfect sentences.

More likely, you would need time to remember how you felt, and decide whether to share such raw feelings with anyone, never mind a stranger who might have a camera or microphone aimed at you.

Some years ago, a Polish woman who had survived Auschwitz hired me to interview her. She was approaching the end of her life and wanted to leave a recording for her adult son, with whom she had a difficult relationship, in the hope he would better understand her.

We recorded her story during several sessions. Often, she would break down and cry. One of those times was a recollection of the day the guards had ordered her to stand in one of two lines of prisoners at Auschwitz. A voice in her head clearly urged her to change lines.

"When the guards weren't looking, I switched," she said. "The line I had been in went to the gas chambers. The one I had gone into went to a labor camp."

When reliving this bittersweet memory, she wept. I did too, but I said nothing. I allowed her to decide whether we should continue. I let the silence guide her deeper into the memory.

What did a moment like that, so incredibly profound, mean to her? To step on such a memory by saying something banal would have been a mistake. "If it's a sad moment, let the moment speak for itself," documentary maker Louis Theroux suggests.

THE DIRECTOR'S CUE

Italian film director Federico Fellini once said, "If there were a little more silence, if we all kept quiet, maybe we could understand something."

KEY TAKEAWAYS

- Silence is full of meaning.
- Many people find silence uncomfortable; don't be one of them.
- Learn not to jump in too soon.

TWENTY-FIVE: **TONE**

In a 2012 interview with Oprah Winfrey, actor Daniel Day-Lewis talked about his lengthy process—he read more than a hundred books—to find the voice of President Abraham Lincoln. It was for the movie *Lincoln*, for which he won his third Academy Award for Best Actor. "The voice is a deep reflection of character, of who we are—the voice is the fingerprint of the soul," he said.

It's also been observed that people might listen to your *words*, but they react to your *tone*. As the famous American wit, Dorothy Parker, once said: "Don't look at me in that tone of voice."

In a *Psychology Today* article, "The Importance of Tone," Dr. Alex Lickerman explored aspects of tone that he, a practicing Buddhist since 1989, had learned:

"Whatever the content of the things we say, it's our tone that communicates what we're feeling when we say them. Our tone tells the truth even when our words don't, even when we're unaware of that truth ourselves. And it's our tone to which others respond. We can even say 'I love you' in a way that provokes bitterness, and then innocently argue we're being unfairly attacked when the person to whom we've said it quite rightly responds to our tone rather than our words.

"Don't be fooled by this kind of faux denial from others. What you think you hear in another person's tone is almost always present. And if someone accuses you of an attitude or feeling you don't think you have, unless they're particularly thick or have some hidden agenda, what they have to say likely represents something you need to hear."

WHY SHOULD INTERVIEWERS CARE ABOUT TONE?

How an interviewer uses tone can influence the outcome of the interview.

Let me offer a painful example. In the early 1980s, I worked with host Peter Gzowski as a producer on the CBC's top national radio program, *Morningside*. Peter had returned to host the program after a hiatus, during which revered Canadian comic Don Harron had taken over. At a story meeting, someone suggested an interview with Don about the famous annual comic review *Spring Thaw*, to which Don had been an important contributor.

I was chosen to line up the item, which everyone at the meeting predicted would be fantastic as it would feature two entertainment giants, Peter and Don. I knew Don a little, as I had worked with him when he hosted.

To prepare a 20-minute live feature—live, because what could go wrong with Peter and Don?—I pre-interviewed Don on the phone to get an idea of the stories he'd want to tell. Then I was to write suggested questions and background notes for Peter.

Things were going great during the pre-talk, until I asked Don for an example of the jokes he told during *Spring Thaw*, which I'd never seen. "Okay," he said. "Something like, 'What do you do when your nose goes on strike? You pick it!'"

I should have laughed or said something positive. But no. I said, in what I must admit was a sarcastic tone, "Are you serious?" To which the entertainer, who was the master of bad jokes and puns, replied: "That's what I *do*, man!"

The rest of our conversation was tense and cut short. I confirmed when we would call him, live, the next day. As the producer of the segment, it was my responsibility to be in the studio at that time, in case anything went wrong. And it did.

At the appointed time, all attempts to call Don went unanswered. The studio producer was going bonkers, as we had almost a half-hour of airtime slotted for the item, and there was nothing to replace it. Peter was becoming frantic, and an angry Peter was not an animal you wanted on your case.

Everyone in the studio glared at me. "Are you *certain* the telephone number is right?" I was asked repeatedly, in an accusatory tone.

Literally, at the last second, Don answered the phone. My blood pressure, which I'm certain was over 200 at this point, immediately returned to normal, but not for long.

Peter, who always liked to weave day-to-day occurrences into the program, shared his anxiety with Don at the start of the segment. "We thought we wouldn't have you. We kept phoning and you weren't there," he said, or words to that effect. "Oh, yeah, your producer, Paul McLaughlin, gave me the wrong time," Don replied, deliberately hanging me out to dry.

I hadn't made a mistake. This was payback, and I deserved it. My tone during the nose-picking anecdote had sealed my fate. I'd sneered at something that mattered to Don. As I scoffed, he plotted revenge. I hope today I'd not react like such a snotty brat in a similar situation.

NO ONE LIKES THE SOUND OF THEIR OWN VOICE

Nothing exemplifies how disconnected we are from our own tone than the aversion most people have to hearing their own voice, sometimes known as "voice confrontation."

A 2018 article in *The Guardian* offered this explanation for the phenomenon. "Because we normally hear our own voice while talking, we receive both sound transferred to our ears externally by air conduction and sound transferred internally through our bones. This bone conduction of sound delivers rich low frequencies that are not included in air-conducted vocal sound. So, when you hear your recorded voice without these frequencies, it sounds higher—and different. Basically, the reasoning is that because our recorded voice does not sound how we expect it to, we don't like it."

The last sentence says it all: most of us don't know how we sound. So, how likely is it that we're aware of, and in control of, our tone, especially when we're stressed?

Haven't most of us said the following at some point during a conversation or argument: "Don't talk to me in that tone of voice." The wrong tone can start all sorts of conflict. For example, the word "fine" can sound benign or sarcastic depending on tone.

TONE AND MEANING MUST MATCH

"In his 1971 book, Silent Messages, *Albert Mehrabian, Professor Emeritus of Psychology at UCLA and influential researcher in the field of*

> *nonverbal communication, says when there is a mismatch between a speaker's words and tone, most of the time, people will trust what they sense in the tone over the actual words."*
>
> *Greg Zlevor, who's served as a facilitator with Fortune 50 companies, wrote the above in a 2018 article, "The Power of Tone."*
>
> *"This means tone has the power to shut down communication, trust, confidence, agreement, and possibilities."*

Tone is more likely to cause problems when an interviewer is nervous, ill-prepared, frightened, or presented with a response they don't like, accept, or admire. It's impossible to eliminate this kind of reaction entirely—as Rag'n'Bone Man sings, "We're only human, after all."—but we can reduce the chances of it happening through effective preparation.

A KILLER CONFESSES

> *On a Sunday afternoon in early February 2010, Colonel Russell Williams, commander of Canada's busiest air transport base, Canadian Forces Base (CFB) Trenton, was asked to come to Ottawa Police headquarters to help investigate the murder of 37-year-old Marie France Comeau.*
>
> *She was a military traffic technician who had worked at the base. What Williams didn't know was that the Ontario Provincial Police had compelling evidence linking him to the disappearance and likely*

murder of another woman, Jessica Lloyd, who lived near CFB Trenton. They also believed he had killed Comeau and was responsible for numerous break-ins and sexual assaults in the vicinity of the base.

Ten hours later, Williams had confessed to both murders and told police where they would find Lloyd's body. This was due to a quiet, methodical, and brilliant interview, conducted by Ontario Provincial Police Det. Sgt Jim Smyth. "[It's] one of the best interviews I've ever seen," a police colleague told reporters afterwards.

Williams was subsequently found guilty of both murders, as well as several sexual assaults and other related crimes. He received two life sentences.

The interview shows how even the most horrible acts can be probed in a calm tone. It's on the Internet and well worth watching. I also suggest a fifth estate *segment, on YouTube, entitled "The Confession," hosted by Bob McKeown, where experts analyze Smyth's techniques.*

KEY TAKEAWAYS

- Actor Daniel Day-Lewis says the voice is the finger-print of the soul.
- We often communicate more by tone than by words.
- Inappropriate tones tend to come out when we're nervous or ill-prepared.

TWENTY-SIX: **ONE QUESTION AT A TIME**

I was once invited to talk about interviewing to a high school journalism class. A student had been selected to ask me a list of questions on behalf of the class.

He opened with a kind introduction, then rhymed off all the questions on his list, more than ten.

I desperately tried to retain the list in my head, but with limited success. After having answered as best as I could, I gently noted it was difficult to remember them all.

"One question at a time is the best approach," I said. "However, interviewers with many years of experience often make this mistake, so you're in good company."

I wasn't soft-pedaling to make the nervous young man feel better. I was telling the truth, based on countless observations of media interviews.

Here are some reasons to avoid a double-barreled or multi-barreled question:

- Interviewees tend to answer only the last question posed. The other(s) are often never addressed.
- It allows interviewees to take control, by choosing which question(s) to ignore.
- Depending on the question, it might be unclear which one is being answered. For example: "Are you planning to lock out your employees if they

don't settle and, if so, will you bring in replacement workers?" If the answer is "Probably," does it apply to both questions?

- If the interviewee answers all your questions, which might take some time, an opportunity to explore one of the answers in greater detail could be lost.
- After answering one of your questions, the interviewee may ask you to repeat the other(s). If you can't, it will be embarrassing.

There is an exception to this one-at-a-time rule. In a scrum or news conference, if you've just one chance to pose a question, a double-barreled question is permissible. Just don't be surprised if only one is answered.

KEY TAKEAWAY:

- The golden rule: one question at a time.

TWENTY-SEVEN: OPEN AND CLOSED QUESTIONS

When I was being vetted for the position as CBC's interviewing trainer, I was stunned by a question posed by one of the executives I'd be reporting to: "I just want to make sure you agree with us that you'll tell all the people you train that they should never ask a close-ended question, just open-ended ones."

"Absolutely not," I said.

"Why? Don't you agree open-ended questions are best?"

"I do. But not always. By the way, you asked me a closed-ended question about not asking closed-ended questions."

I then learned that my predecessor had convinced management, for reasons I cannot fathom, to let him impose this restriction on the participants who took his sessions. Imagine telling reporters covering a possible strike they couldn't ask a union leader, "Will you walk off the job tomorrow?" That's just one of countless examples.

Fortunately, I won the day and promised, in all sincerity, to advocate for open-ended questions. In most cases, they provide the best responses as they don't require a yes-or-no answer.

"I think when you ask open-ended questions, that's always going to elicit a better answer or a better response than a closed-ended [one]," American journalist and journalism professor Dean Nelson said in an interview.

"For example, 'Where were you born?'—well, I could say Chicago—as opposed to, 'What was it like growing up in Chicago?' If you're a good interviewer, you already know that I was born in Chicago. You've done your homework. Ask it in some way that will draw the person out as opposed to just kind of one-word answers."

However, Nelson cautioned that some questions can be too open-ended. "I use the example of after some sort of phenomenal Olympic achievement, somebody has just done something that's never been done before, and an interviewer will say, 'What does it feel like?' Well, that's so open-ended, it doesn't feel like anything."

The Poynter Institute agrees that "the best questions are open-ended. They begin with how, what, where, when, why. They're conversation starters and encourage expansive answers that produce an abundance of information needed to produce a complete and accurate story. Closed-ended questions are more limited, but they have an important purpose. Ask them when you need a direct answer: 'Did you embezzle the company's money?' Closed-ended questions put people on the record."

Both types of questions have merit. Consider the rationale I offered in my training sessions: "Ask what you think is the best question, be it open or closed. Don't fall back on formulas and don't believe everything a trainer tells you, myself included."

KEY TAKEAWAY

- Open-ended questions are preferred to closed ones, but the latter often must be employed.

TWENTY-EIGHT: **FOLLOWING UP ON ANSWERS**

One of the keys to effective interviewing? Don't just ask questions. Follow up on answers.

Too many interviewers have a list of questions they seem to think are the only ones they need to ask. That's a serious mistake. As an interview unfolds, you'll have to decide whether to explore an answer further or move on to a new line of questioning. Often, it's the former.

Some people, either naturally or because they were media-trained (instructed to keep answers brief), tend to provide short answers. A few will volunteer lengthy and highly detailed responses.

But many will not.

It's also not human nature to offer every detail in the first response to a question. For example, if you ask a person what it was like to have survived a mugging, and the answer is, "It was traumatic," you need to explore what "traumatic" means in this context.

Q: I can understand that it must have been. Would you be able to explain in what way it was traumatic? Or,

Q: Can you go into more detail? Or,

Q: Do you have anything to compare it to?

Many more follow-up questions could ensue. They're usually a variation of "tell me more" or "what did you mean."

You often have to slowly elicit the details that further explain an important area of questioning, while gently trying to help the person evoke their emotions at the time (depending on the topic). And, as always, you're hoping to obtain anecdotes that enhance the storytelling.

For print interviews, the details are critical and will help you recreate what happened when you write your story. They are also important for broadcast but, often, the emotions will provide the most powerful audience reactions.

KEEP ASKING

Every answer can be plumbed to go a step further, says Pulitzer Prize-winning writer Jacqui Banaszyski, if the reporter is listening for promising nuggets and willing to linger on them: "For every answer you get, ask five more questions. The first answer will probably be very general. Stay in the moment and peel it back."

KEY TAKEAWAY

- The real art in interviewing is knowing when, and how, to follow up on answers.

TWENTY-NINE: **COMING UP WITH THE NEXT QUESTION**

One of the hardest skills a new interviewer needs to acquire is the ability to listen to an answer and have the next question at the ready. It's more of a challenge in broadcast interviews, where your silence could be uncomfortable for the guest and audience, but it happens during print interviews as well.

I know from personal experience, especially early in my career, how difficult that can be. There were times on assignment for CBC Radio that I could barely breathe as an answer seemed to be winding down and I had no idea what I was going to ask next. It felt as if I was drowning.

An unfortunate remedy is to start babbling inanely as you desperately search for a new question. Some guests, sensing your struggle, will step in and help you out; others will wait until you've arrived at some semblance of a question, perhaps even enjoying your predicament, no matter how many agonizing moments it takes.

If it happens to you, let me assure you it gets less frequent with experience; the challenge might still arise, but you tend to know ways to deal with it, sometimes by not being afraid to use a brief silence or by throwing out a generic question that follows up on the answer ("Can you go into greater detail?" or "What was your thinking behind that?" etc.).

If all options fail, you can always tell the truth: "I'm sorry, I've lost my train of thought" or "My mind has gone blank. Can you remind me what we were just talking about?" It might be painful to admit, especially for a broadcast interview, but it should do the trick.

KEY TAKEAWAY

- It can be difficult (and often terrifying) not to have the next question at the ready, but it gets easier to deal with the more experienced you become.

THIRTY: **D&A, THE LIFEBLOOD OF FEATURES**

D&A is a mnemonic I created as a reminder of what to obtain in some interviews. D for details, A for anecdotes. These are the DNA of good storytelling.

Often, an interviewer gets into what I call a riff with the interviewee, especially if they're making a positive connection. Bland feedback such as "yeah," "for sure," "absolutely" are fine in a conversation with a friend, but they can be detrimental in an interview. They reinforce what the other person is saying rather than assessing, exploring, and possibly challenging the answers.

If you catch yourself riffing rather than interviewing during a print interview, I suggest you do a quick mental check to assess whether you understand what the person said well enough to write about it in detail and with some color.

For broadcast, when you engage in this kind of meaningless feedback to an answer, you might miss a chance to follow up and explore an answer in greater detail.

DETAILS

Here's an example of riffing. Imagine this interview with someone whose airplane crashed in the North, in frigid weather:

Q: What was it like?

A: My God it was cold. I couldn't believe how bad it was.

Q: For sure. I can really understand.

A: I've never experienced anything like that.

Q: It must have been horrible.

A: You have no idea.

Q: I can imagine.

Nothing wrong with any of that, except for the absence of any usable details.

Here's a possible D&A version:

A: My God it was cold. I couldn't believe how bad it was.

Q: Do you have any sense of how cold it actually was?

A: I'm not certain but the thermometer on the plane said minus 35.

Q: Fahrenheit or Celsius?

A: Fahrenheit.

Q: I can't imagine. What did that feel like in your body?

A: I've never experienced anything like it.

Q: Can you compare it to anything?

A: It felt like my bones had frozen solid. No matter how cold you've ever felt, it was a hundred times worse.

Details such as these will bring a story to life.

SPECIFICS

Interviewers need to elicit specifics. If someone says a building is "tall," what does that mean? Is it three storeys high? A hundred?

If someone says "an older" person walked into a room, how old is old? The answer likely has something to do with the age of the speaker.

What does tall mean to someone who's 5'4"? Or 6'3"? The only way to find the answers is to ask.

ANECDOTES

We need stories because we're in the business of storytelling. That seems obvious, but interviewers often fail to elicit anecdotes.

There's nothing memorable or compelling about most basic information, even though you might need it for your article or broadcast. Yarns, events, and incidents add color and context, and will engage the reader or audience. People love stories. It's your job to coax them from the person you're interviewing.

No matter how hard you try, some interviewees inherently are not good storytellers. That's not a defect; it's a characteristic. If you encounter a poor storyteller, don't get upset. It's just the way the person is. Rather, look for other possible interviewees on the same topic.

However, if you do find yourself in the company of someone who can spin a yarn, exploit that gift for all it's worth.

If you realize there's an engaging anecdote you might use—I call this "the gold" or "the pixie dust"—slow down and meticulously walk the person through the story.

For example, imagine someone tells you they had an awful car accident on the way to a crucial meeting. Here are questions you might ask for a print interview:

At what time did you leave your house? What was your destination? What kind of vehicle were you driving? Were you alone in the car? What route had you planned? Do you know exactly when it happened? Where did it happen? What happened? What other vehicles were involved? Do you know what type of vehicle hit you? Did the police arrive? Did they talk to you? If so, what was said?

As you're asking the questions, you should be assessing whether you have enough information to reconstruct the scene, point by point.

For broadcast, you'll likely ask far fewer questions. You might focus on one aspect of the event and concentrate your questions in that area, making sure to explore what the person was feeling as the accident occurred.

Don't race through the events. Take your time and slowly piece together a picture of what happened. If the person is doing a good job of recounting what occurred, don't interrupt the flow, unless you absolutely have to. If there are points you need to follow up on, jot them down and ask them later.

For interviews about traumatic events, past or present, be aware the person could be in shock or suffering from PTSD. Make sure the interviewee is comfortable being questioned. Talking about a traumatic event can be cathartic for some interviewees; for others, it could be harrowing to relive the experience.

Some people need active prompts to tell a story in detail: Can you give me an example? Please explain. Go on. Continue. What do you mean? Is there a story behind what you're saying? If this was a movie pitch, how would you tell the story?

In the 2020 miniseries *The Comey Rule*, both FBI Director James Comey and Deputy Director Andrew McCabe used "say more" to elicit details and anecdotes from people they were questioning. Our version is "tell me more."

The broadcaster Stuart McLean said that when he spoke with nervous people, he'd begin an answer for them. For example, with a bank teller who was robbed, but too afraid to describe what happened, he might start off like this: "So when the man walked into the bank and you looked at him, after that you..." and let the person continue. A fragmented question also works: "You would describe the person as..."

All these questions or prompts are techniques to keep a person talking, which is one of an interviewer's most important functions.

Why so much emphasis on D&A? In addition to painting mental pictures, details provide credibility, color, and authenticity to your reporting.

And anecdotes? Who doesn't love a great story? A story shows rather than tells, which is a vital resource for any good journalist. It's fine to say a person is a coward. But if you have a scene in which the person runs away rather than fights, it says so much more.

Actions reveals character. Don't tell me a man is a womanizer. Show me the man trying to seduce a woman.

If you encourage storytelling, it increases the potential that the interviewee will try to accommodate your needs. In fact, I often mention to the interviewee before we begin that any examples they can recall will be especially helpful. This doesn't always result in them providing useful anecdotes, but it sometimes does.

For broadcast, if you know the person has a great anecdote to tell (through your research or from info provided by a booker), encourage the person to tell that story once the recording has begun. Some might forget, or just decide not to, but my experience is that many will try to accommodate this reasonable request.

I also ask them not to say, "As we talked about earlier," or any similar wording. If you don't, you risk the possibility they will tell the audience the anecdote has been somewhat staged.

LOOK FOR CONNECTIONS

A few years ago, during a media junket in Finland, I was part of a group of international journalists interviewing a woman who'd founded a company that created clothing for burn victims.

After she'd answered some general questions about her business, it struck me to ask if she had a personal reason for establishing her company.

Indeed she had.

Her son had suffered terrible burns when he was young and this inspired her to help others. What she told us was emotional and inspiring and so different in wording and tone from the meat-and-potato answers we'd been given up to that point

This information wasn't on any background sheets we'd been given on the company, which is sometimes the case.

Always ask yourself if there might be connections between what a person does and the motivation behind it.

KEY TAKEAWAYS

- Details and anecdotes are the lifeblood of feature stories.
- One of our tasks is to keep a person talking when they're discussing important matters.
- Always look for the motivation behind a major decision, such as starting a company, changing jobs, etc.

THIRTY-ONE: **SLOW DOWN**

When I was the CBC's interviewing trainer, I asked participants at the end of a course what advice had resonated the most. My sessions typically lasted three to five days, so we'd covered a lot of ground by that point.

By far, my recommendation to "slow down" during an interview received the most votes.

What does that mean?

Having analyzed many interviews over the years—including my own—I noticed many of them were rushed.

Some interviewers are far too hyped, too eager to interject, and jump in too soon with a new question. This might happen as the interviewee is wrapping up an answer or, more concerningly, before the interviewee has finished an answer.

This can sometimes cut off a potentially important piece of information. People rarely provide concise and complete answers. By cutting them off, the pixie dust may blow away.

Sometimes, you have to let an answer breathe. Take a moment, even if only a few seconds, to let the person's answer come to a full stop. Don't feel as if you have to flex your interviewing muscles immediately. Take your time.

Many interviewers, especially broadcasters, are disconcerted by silence. The latter fear what is called dead air, when no obvious sound is being heard by the audience. I was taught to avoid it and, like many others, suffered from the "dead air dream," which I've learned is common in the profession.

Robert MacNeil, former co-host of *The MacNeil/Lehrer Report* on PBS, says this paranoia is unwarranted: "The hardest thing to do in television is to listen to the answers. The reason is that the interviewer, from his earliest experience, has a terror of dead air, that the answer will be brief and he won't have another question ready. So, to cover himself, he starts looking at and getting ready with the next question on his list, almost the minute he's finished asking the one preceding. Just watch interviews very closely on television, and how, before the camera cuts to the interviewee, you'll often see the interviewer's eyes drop to the page right after asking the question.

"The difficulty of listening is that you're taking the risk that listening may produce a more interesting question. It might give rise to 'Oh, what do you really mean by that?' and a little bit of dead air for a minute. Frankly, we don't care, Lehrer and I, about a little dead air. We'd rather be caught musing for a moment and saying, 'Gee, that's interesting. I hadn't thought about that. Let me see, what do I want to ask you next?'"

But silence is not actually an absence of sound or meaning. Fred Jacobs, founder of Jacobs Media, wrote about "The Power of Dead Air" in a 2018 article. He argued, correctly in my opinion, that pauses and silence can be powerful moments in an interview.

"One of the best purveyors of the pause was [NPR's] *All Things Considered* maestro, Robert Siegel," Jacobs wrote. "He had the ability to turn a phrase, but also use moments of silence as a tool to keep your attention riveted on the important topics and issues of the day, on the drive home.

"When you see a great standup comic or a brilliant orator in person, those calculated moments of silence provide time for the audience to react. Great personality radio often amounts to compelling storytelling. And stories that draw you in need to be delivered in ways that give you pause—that make you think, respond, and emote."

INTERVIEWING ELDERLY PEOPLE

The elderly can be particularly perturbed by an antsy interviewer.

A 2014 study by the School of Psychological Sciences, University of Northern Colorado, noted that, "Older age produces numerous changes in cognitive processes, including slowing in the rate of mental processing speed." I have no idea what age constitutes "older," but in my experience, it's wise to offer more time and space for answers when interviewing someone around the age of 75 or older.

Some interviewers step in, cut the elderly person off, and finish answering the question for them because they perceive the person to be a little senile. This is a serious mistake. You might be squelching what could have been a remarkable response, and your impatience—in words or body language—might annoy the interviewee and shut them down.

None of this is to say, by any means, that you should never interrupt or jump in. There are numerous times when you must. But make it a decision, not a habit.

THE SPEED OF STRESS

Stress, of course, can contribute to some interviewers being too speedy. And interviewing, to say the least, can be stressful. Unfortunately, when we rush, we're likely not functioning at our highest capacity, and it heightens the potential to miss something important.

"We learn to become more empathic when we slow down, become present, and are fully committed to understanding another person's uniqueness," says Arthur Ciaramicoli, a U.S. clinical psychologist and author of *The Stress Solution: Using Empathy and Cognitive Behavioral Therapy to Reduce Anxiety and Develop Resilience.*

Being present in an interview, however, is easier said than accomplished. With so many distractions, especially for a broadcast piece, taking your time can be challenging.

The speed at which much journalism takes place these days contributes to the tendency to gallop through an interview. A 2017 article on the *National Geographic* website about the new "slow journalism" movement encourages journalists to resist the mounting compulsion to always be first when reporting.

"In today's newsrooms, pressure to publish stories at an increasingly fast rate often means that reporters are able to uncover only basic information and complete a surface-level analysis," Australian freelance writer Matt Norman says in the article. "Twenty years ago, media experts were already warning that working at high speeds encourages journalists 'to fall back on well-worn themes and observations—interpretive clichés.' In today's world of digital media, this effect has been compounded."

I think that impetus also applies to interviews.

Try to take your time when exploring something interesting or important with a guest. By slowing down, you have a greater chance of hearing what a person is actually saying, and of formulating a meaningful response. As American singer Eddie Cantor once said, "Slow down and enjoy life. It's not only the scenery you miss by going too fast, you also miss the sense of where you are going and why."

KEY TAKEAWAYS

- Slowing down is one of the most important, but least known, requirements of interviewing.
- It helps you listen to the answers and allows the interviewee a chance to add to their response.
- The slow journalism movement encourages journalists to resist the compulsion to always be first when reporting.

THIRTY-TWO: DON'T ANSWER YOUR OWN QUESTIONS

When hockey hall-of-famer Dale Hawerchuk died of cancer in 2020, at age 57, a Toronto sports radio program asked one of its contributors, Brian Burke, the former NHL executive, to speak about the well-liked player and coach.

The host, who is good at his demanding job, began by listing about five or six of Hawerchuk's positive personality traits. Then he asked Burke what he thought. "That's exactly what I would have said," Burke replied.

In hindsight, I'm sure the host would have preferred to hear Burke provide those insights, but it was a friendly broadcast segment and worked out okay. Imagine if that had been a print interview. One of the most important questions would not have elicited anything quotable.

Answering for the person is by no means a trait exclusive to sports interviews. I observe it all the time.

As noted previously, there are times when "forcing a card," as I like to call it—putting words into the guest's mouth—can be beneficial, if not essential. On investigative programs, such as *60 Minutes* or *Dateline*, notice how the interviewer may feed an interviewee the words to use.

For example, "I imagine when you found this out you were really shocked and felt betrayed." To which the interviewee replies, "Yes. I was really shocked and, yes, I felt betrayed."

Is there anything wrong with this? Yes and no.

On the positive side, it can be difficult to shape a broadcast segment, especially if time is tight. Some guests might not be able to articulate concise responses that the program, through its research, believes to exist. Or that the interviewer intuits. So why not help? Guests have the right to offer different answers if they don't agree with the menu presented to them. This technique can also be used for news reports, where time pressure can be intense.

On the negative side, when people are nervous—and being interviewed, especially for a national TV segment, can elicit that emotion—some tend to buy time by using the words presented to them in a question as the beginning of their answer. Or they might sense that the interviewer is not open or interested in the truth and may go along with the proposed wording to appease rather than confront.

When I first started in journalism, the radio program I worked on engaged a freelancer who was exceptionally good at getting interviewees to say the exact words she wanted them to use. Her grating personality contributed to her success.

If she wanted an interviewee to use the word "upset," for example, she'd ask repeatedly whether the person was upset: "Are you upset? I mean, I'd be upset!" "Surely you're upset!" "You can't tell me you're not upset!"

The person inevitably would blurt out an answer that included confirmation or denial of being upset. If they said they weren't, they usually did so in such an aggravated tone, in reaction to her badgering, that suggested they actually were upset. The freelancer would then edit the tape and cut out her barrage of prompts.

The UK PR firm Media First lists this technique in its "Journalist Tricks and Traps: 10 Types of Questions to Prepare for Before an Interview." It's # 3: Putting words into your mouth.

"Journalists will sometimes use negative phrases in their questions. Very often the interviewee repeats this negative language, even when they are defending themselves and rebutting the accusation. For example, you might be asked: 'This is very disappointing isn't it? Aren't you disappointed?' You answer: 'I wouldn't say it's disappointing...' But you just have. The journalist's negative language can now be attributed to you."

A variation on this technique is to offer guests two possible answers, as if they're the only ones worth considering.

For example: "Would you say your company's decision was made with great consideration or in haste?" Now that's a fine question if those are indeed the only two possible choices, but what if they're not? Or, worse, what if the decision was made in haste, but the interviewee has now been given an option to say it was done with great consideration, which would surely make the interviewee look better? If it's possible to counter this with evidence of a hasty process, that would be fine, but that's often not the case.

Here's the problem with this tactic: What if the person would have answered differently if they'd been asked an open question, one that didn't contain any trigger wording? It's best to ask the interviewee for a reaction, not to tell them what it is.

THE RIGHT WAY TO DO IT

A wonderful example of what can be gained by allowing a guest to answer, rather than assuming what they would say, happened on *Metro Morning*, the Toronto CBC Radio program, perhaps in the mid-1990s (I'm fuzzy on the date). Reporter Jean Kim was contributing to a series on victims of gun violence by introducing us to Gordon (a pseudonym). He'd been shot and paralyzed in a drive-by shooting, where he was an innocent bystander.

Kim attended Gordon's graduation ceremony where he was to receive a degree or diploma in civil engineering, I believe.

Most interviewers, in such an emotionally charged moment, would have been tempted to supply an answer for the interviewee ("You must have been so proud..." "It must have been an incredible sense of accomplishment...") and waited for Gordon to confirm the response.

But Kim didn't. She asked him what it was like for him that day. I recall him saying it was one of the worst days of his life because he now had a colostomy bag and the ceremony, like all graduations, took forever and the bag was full, and he was sore from sitting in his wheelchair for such a long time.

I was listening in my kitchen and his comments broke my heart; but they also had me cheering the interviewer. Her open question elicited a specific, powerful answer I'll never forget.

If you intend to present an interviewee with a possible answer, the most important point to consider beforehand is whether you're certain it's an accurate one. Don't assume. If you're uncertain, just ask. The answer might even surprise you.

KEY TAKEAWAY

- Putting words into an interviewee's mouth can often work to your advantage, but it's not always the right (or best) thing to do.

THIRTY-THREE: **INTERVIEWEE FATIGUE**

When Eva Avila won the 2006 singing contest *Canadian Idol*, she did 74 media interviews in the first three days after her win. Imagine the similarity of the questions. "What does it feel like," probably topped the list. Avila was only 19, and new to the interview game. It was likely enjoyable, but tiring, to be in such demand.

Many film and TV stars, athletes, and other oft-interviewed celebrities might have a different reaction. They're often asked the same few questions repeatedly, year after year after year. At some point it has to get tiring.

I call it interviewee fatigue. Think about it before engaging with a famous person.

You might have experienced something similar. If you've ever worn a cast, or had a black eye, remember how you first responded to the inevitable inquiries. You may have provided lots of detail at first and might have even embellished the story somewhat.

Then it became tedious.

When weariness kicks in, many people condense the story, as I remember doing after I broke my ankle in 2019 on Valentine's Day. The date is a detail I always mentioned in my early account of what had happened, but after a week or so, my synopsis was something like, "Yeah, I slipped on some ice in my driveway, and it broke. No big deal."

Not all celebrities display annoyance at an interviewer's lack of originality. For example, singer Tony Bennett seems to approach each interview with enthusiasm and energy, as if he'd never been asked about "I Left My Heart in San Francisco."

Others, like the ultra-private Beyoncé or the notoriously testy Harrison Ford, avoid most interviews or reluctantly agree to them. Ford is known for giving "yes" or "no" answers, an interviewer's bane. He particularly dislikes promoting a new movie. "I've always been an independent son of a bitch, so if I'm grumpy, then call me grumpy. I'm all right with that," he's said.

Movie junkets, as they're called, don't appeal to many film stars. Typically, the film's studio flies reporters into Los Angeles, New York, or Toronto, puts them up at a lovely hotel, and screens the movie. Soon after, the journalists gather in small groups in several rooms and the studio brings in the stars, the director, and perhaps other prominent members of the production team for a round-table group chat on a rotating basis.

TV interviewers might have one-on-one access to the top stars, but typically for five minutes or even less. For them, the stars remain in the same room and the journalists are ferreted in and out. The interviewers also have to deal with a system created to benefit the studios: the camera crew and the copy of the interview belong to the studio. The journalists had better behave or risk leaving empty-handed.

"It's a grinding regimen for the stars but also for the journalists, who may cover three or four movies this way in a weekend, if the studios cooperate with each other," Gary Susman wrote in *The Guardian* in 2001.

"As a freelance newspaper journalist and film critic, I've attended hundreds of junkets over the years, though I'm not one of the 200 or so road warriors who attend them virtually every weekend."

In 1999, Ralph Benmergui, then host of CBC TV's *Midday*, was assigned to just such a junket, which took place at a Toronto hotel. He was scheduled to interview John Travolta, who was starring in a new movie, *The General's Daughter*. Benmergui did not like the film, nor did he like asking what he calls "process questions" about the making of the film—typically, questions such as, "What was it like working with…" "How did you prepare for…"

Just before the interview started, he was told his time had been cut from five to three minutes. What to do in such a short timespan?

Fortunately, Benmergui had prepared for the interview. "I try to find what makes an artist, or entertainer, tick," he says. "I'd read background articles on Travolta and learned he'd recently shot two films in Vancouver and had flown his own jet to get there. He was a well-known Scientologist, who flew to his summer home [in Maine]. His neighbor there was [actor] Kirstie Alley, another Scientologist."

When Benmergui was ushered in for the interview, Travolta appeared exhausted and disinterested. Until Benmergui's first question: "What's it like flying into Vancouver?"

Travolta's body language almost immediately changed. He'd been slumped in his chair but now sat up. "It's fantastic," he began. "You come in over the water and the lights…it's beautiful."

Benmergui then asked why Travolta liked to barnstorm Kirstie Alley's house in his plane? He was given another enthusiastic answer.

Next: "What's an assist?" referring to a common Scientology practice. Travolta was used to journalists confronting him about the controversial religion, so he cautiously asked Benmergui whether he genuinely wanted to know. When assured he did, Travolta explained it was a healing method that he sometimes used on Alley.

By this point, the studio's handler was giving the wrap sign. Benmergui continued nonetheless: "What effect has having millions of dollars had on your ability to form friendships?" he asked. Upon hearing that question, Travolta waved off the wrap sign. "That is one of the best questions I have had to date," he said, and proceeded to give a thoughtful answer.

Benmergui got a copy of the tape.

POETIC INJUSTICE

Here's an example of interviewee fatigue, where the subject of the interview off-loaded the problem. The legendary beat poet Allen Ginsberg agreed to an interview with two students who were working on a thesis about his work, but with one ominous caveat: "As long as you don't ask me anything I've been asked before."

Former U.S. public radio host Dan Moulthrop shared this story in a 2015 TED Talk. He was one of the students. Moulthrop and a university colleague stayed up all night, sifting through material about the poet, trying to meet his constraint. "I mean, the dude

> had been interviewed a lot," Moulthrop said. It worked
> out, he told the audience, without offering details.
>   I can't imagine how challenging that must have
> been and salute the two of them for successfully
> conducting such a tough interview.

WHAT IF YOU HAVE TO ASK TIRED, OLD QUESTIONS?

Sometimes, if an editor or producer has mandated a certain approach to a story, it's necessary to cover old ground.

What to do?

For a print piece, I'll search for an article or video in which the classic stories are discussed. If the interviewee knows the source I'm referencing, I'll ask whether I can I use those quotes for my piece, to save them from answering the same, old questions. No one has refused.

This approach can elicit surprising information. When working on a magazine profile of Wayne Gretzky when he was a young hockey star, I came across an article in which he was quoted saying, "I'd rather live one day as a lion than 100 years as a sheep."

I'd spent time with the affable, but not (yet) eloquent, young hockey star and felt certain he'd never say something like that. When I interviewed the feisty Peter Pocklington, then owner of the Edmonton Oilers, the team Gretzky played for, I threw the quote at him. "Wayne never said that!" Pocklington yelled into the phone. "I said that!" I believed him.

The moral? Not everything you read is accurate.

If I must ask interviewees to retell old stories, they appreciate it when I warn them. I'll say, "I know many of our readers/viewers won't have heard them. If you're okay to visit them again, I'll try to make my questions sound fresh."

I've had positive reactions to this request. Almost all seem to appreciate the courtesy and respect that I believe are inherent in me acknowledging that it can be a drag to go over old territory.

KEY TAKEAWAYS

- Imagine what it must be like to be asked the same questions year after year. Can you come up with an approach to overcome this problem?
- If you have to ask an oft-posed question, consider first discussing with the interviewee why you have to do this.
- Don't trust everything you read about a public figure; if it doesn't sound like something they'd say, check it out.

THIRTY-FOUR: **THE BROADCAST INTERVIEW**

In early July 1995, British actor Hugh Grant appeared on *The Tonight Show with Jay Leno*, ostensibly to promote his latest film, *Nine Months*. However, the romantic comedy was not the foremost topic of conversation that night.

Two weeks earlier, Grant had been arrested on Hollywood's Sunset Boulevard, while receiving oral sex in his car from a sex worker. As the audience gave Grant a long and enthusiastic welcome, the always-fidgety actor appeared extremely uncomfortable as he awaited the start of the interview.

"Okay, question number one," Leno said, a smile on his large face. "What the hell were you thinking?"

The studio band helped punctuate the moment with a brief drum roll. The audience howled. Grant's stammering answer didn't really matter. The question broke the tension in the room and managed to be on point and funny at the same time. Whoever came up with it—perhaps Leno himself—hit the perfect note.

That interview propelled NBC into a ratings lead in the late-night talk show wars, besting David Letterman at CBS for the first time.

The first question in a broadcast interview is far more important than one for a print interview.

I can't imagine starting a broadcast interview without knowing what I'm going to ask first.

Sometimes, opening questions need to be provocative to reflect what's on a listener's or viewer's mind.

For example, Americans were intensely curious about Monica Lewinsky, who had an affair with President Bill Clinton while he was in office. In 1999, Barbara Walters of ABC's *20/20* opened her interview with this: "Monica, you have been described as a bimbo, a stalker, a seductress. Describe yourself."

To which the unfairly maligned Lewinsky replied, after a deep sigh, "I think I'm very loving, very loyal. I think I'm very intelligent..."

These were not likely the first words the two had exchanged before the cameras began rolling, but it was a powerful, concise way to start, and it was fair comment.

Diane Sawyer used a similar approach in her ABC interview with Whitney Houston in December 2002, on the heels of the singer's mysterious show cancellations, erratic behavior, and alleged drug abuse: "You know that as we sit here and talk, everyone watching this is going to be staring at you physically and they're going to be saying, 'How thin is she now? How many bones can we see? Is she sick? And how sick is she?'"

To which Houston interjected, in a hushed, croaky voice her publicist attributed to laryngitis, "I'm not sick, Diane. I am not sick. Let's get that straight. I am not sick."

(On February 11, 2012, Houston died of accidental drowning in a bathtub in the Beverly Hills Hilton hotel. The coroner found cocaine and other drugs in her system, including Xanax, at the time. She was 48.)

It was, as so many broadcast interviews require, a dramatic beginning.

SOME FOUNDATION REQUIRED

Some interviews, however, need to start with a foundation question. That's when you ask the guest to explain something the audience has to understand for the rest of the interview to make sense. Sometimes this information can be included in the introduction, but not always.

For example, for an interview with a scientist, you might need to begin with: "I think many people are confused about the difference between global warming and climate change. Can you briefly explain the difference for us?"

For a profile, the best first question could be one that starts at the beginning of the person's career: "What was your first big break?" With a music guest, you might ask: "Do you remember the first time you ever sang in public?" To an athlete: "When did you first think you might be able to play professionally?" or "When you were starting out, who especially supported you?"

It's best if you already know the answer (for broadcast, this can be thanks to your research or a pre-interview conducted by someone else) but that's not always possible. Sometimes you have to gamble that the response will be engaging or meaningful.

The most interesting questions, and the ones that work best for a broadcast interview, are those that elicit an emotional response or tackle a conflict head on.

Questions in search of details often are critical in print interviews, but less so for broadcast.

Obviously, if the interview is taped, and there's time to edit, there is less need to make every question count, but long, rambling, unclear questions can't always be cut out. Nor can you always excise digressions that don't advance the interview.

DAVID FROST ON THE INTERVIEW SUBTEXT

In 1977, David Frost's televised interviews with former President Richard Nixon were so historic they became the basis of a stage play and a major film. Here's how Frost summed up his perception of the TV interview:

"Over the last half century, the television interview has given us some of TV's most heart-stopping and memorable moments. On the surface, it is a simple format—two people sitting across from one another having a conversation. But underneath it is often a power struggle—a battle for the psychological advantage."

THE NEED FOR A DYNAMIC

A memorable broadcast interview is an artful mix of journalism and theater. The interviewer is not just speaking when asking questions but presenting them with the energy of a trained actor.

Although it's inadvisable, a print interviewer can get away with slouching, or speaking in a low, tired voice. A broadcaster needs to be a presence—sitting or standing in an assertive position and enunciating clearly.

Unlike for a print interview, the broadcaster has an audience observing the interaction with the guest. This requires performing the interview, not just conducting it.

Imagine watching a conversation between two people in which neither exudes much energy or enthusiasm. Nor does the interviewer ask any interesting questions or elicit any compelling responses. The encounter produces nothing to hold a viewer's interest. It's all just bland chitchat.

In this day and age, with consumers offered so many viewing choices on their phone alone, the chances are considerable that a deadly dull interview will not hold their attention for long.

If you're just looking for a short clip, perhaps for a news item, you can likely attain your goal even if the interview is uninspiring. But if all, or a significant portion of, the uninteresting interaction is broadcast, it will almost assuredly be a failure.

Consequently, a broadcast interviewer needs to plan an interview with the understanding that the dynamic between themselves and the guest can be a critical aspect of the final product.

In recent years, I've seen that many print reporters, when pressed into conducting video interviews as part of a new job requirement, are (understandably) unaware of the need to project their voice and be in control of how they involve their body, as just two aspects of what the broadcast format demands.

In fact, many experienced broadcasters, if not standing, sit on the edge of their chair to ensure they're alert and have good posture and can breathe effortlessly. Many media trainers tell their clients to sit this way during an office or studio interview.

How important are the physical demands of broadcasting? Ralph Benmergui says that when he was at CBC, he wanted to try his hand at reading a newscast on air. His first go was not a success. "Afterwards, [an established reader] explained to me what I'd done wrong. She said, 'You don't read the news. You *perform* it.' I realized right away that she was right."

You can't speak at the volume you normally use in a broadcast interview (unless you normally talk like a stage actor). Rather, you have to project. This means speaking a bit louder than normal, but without yelling. Just as theater actors have to make sure they're heard at the back of the room, a broadcaster has to keep the needs of the listener or viewer in mind. Mumbling or speaking softly, unless it's a deliberate technique, won't accomplish that well.

THE AUDIENCE

There are three parties to a broadcast interview: the guest, the interviewer, and the audience. Too often, the audience is forgotten, and that's a mistake. If you ask a relevant question but are attacked for asking it, that will be noted; but if you're afraid to ask an essential question, or don't listen well enough to follow-up on an answer, that too will be observed.

Your questions need to be concise and clear. Remember that, in most cases, the audience is listening to the interview as it's being presented live or on tape. If something is unclear, there's nothing they can do in the moment to rectify that. They should be able to take another look at it later on, if it's posted, but the initial impression will have been damaged if something didn't make sense.

Also keep the theatrical element in mind as the interview unfolds. Just as in a play, whatever takes place has to make sense. That means you can't (or shouldn't) abruptly change direction in the interview unless you bridge the change as part of your next question, such as, "I wonder if we could now discuss…" or, "Because I have limited time and there's so much I want to explore, perhaps we could now talk about…" or words to that effect.

Time management more often is a factor in a broadcast interview, especially if the interview is live. The host of a live morning radio program, for example, typically has three to seven minutes for an interview. Time can't be wasted on general questions to warm up the guest.

No matter how much time is available, it's your responsibility (and that of a producer, if one is assigned to you) to accomplish your goals in whatever time exists.

Another responsibility is knowing how and when to interrupt. If the guest is rambling and time is evaporating, you have to interrupt and shift the direction of the interview, and you need to do it with style and grace.

Some interviewees, by the way, have been trained to provide protracted answers to eat up time in an interview they anticipate might have a confrontational element. If that occurs, knowing how to interrupt becomes even more important.

It's smart to know, and practice, how to end an interview. For example: "This has been extremely helpful/interesting/important and I just want to thank you so much for your time/insights/energy…"

You will likely develop your own exit phrases but it's beneficial to have one or more possibilities at the ready.

One approach is to play off the last answer as a bridge to your wrapping-up comment. For example: "I think that's a wonderful note on which to end. Thank you so much." Some interviewers use a "trademark" phrase, such as one CBC host who ended almost every interview with, "It was a pleasure to meet you on the radio."

BE TOTALLY PRESENT

All interviews, but especially broadcast ones, require you to listen at an almost preternatural level. Journalist Warner Troyer, who worked on television public affairs programs such as This Hour Has Seven Days, the fifth estate, *and* W5, *described his interviewing experience like this:*

"I'm burning so much adrenaline everything is happening in slow motion for me. And that means I have masses of time to listen to what is being said, to watch the way it's being said, and to judge the temperature and barometric pressure, intellectually and emotionally, of the person I'm talking to.

"Based on all of that information and on my imperatives—the things I want to get done and the amount of time left—I can then determine what kind of question I should ask next, what the tone of it should be, whether I should smile or look rather stern, whether I should lean back or forward.

"It's not just that you have to be there—the rest of the world does not exist. You're in a submarine, a bathysphere, alone with that individual. And you force them to attend to you and only you. And you do force them, with eye contact, with the urgency of your interest in them, all these things."

OFF-CAMERA INTERVIEWS

In 2007, when I worked on Fraud Squad TV,

my role was to conduct all the interviews without appearing on camera, visually or verbally. A studio host later voiced a script that set up the clips we used on air.

There are several challenges in these situations:

Ask questions in a way that guides interviewees to answer in full sentences. I often coached guests, for these types of interviews, to repeat my question as the start of their answer. If I asked, for example, when they were born, I'd suggest they begin their response with, "I was born…"

It's especially important to avoid yes/no questions. Open-ended questions are best, such as "Tell me about…" or "Please go over what happened that day…"

Avoid verbal listening or interjections. Verbal listening is where an interviewer, usually out of habit or nervousness, tries to encourage the guest by saying, "right," or "yeah" or "really?" In general, this is distracting for the viewer or listener. In off-camera interviews, it's verboten.

KEY TAKEAWAYS

- Broadcast interviews require you to perform the interview.
- The first question is often the most important.
- Avoid verbal listening during a broadcast interview.

THIRTY-FIVE: **THE PRINT INTERVIEW**

I recognize this is stating the obvious: the primary difference between a print and broadcast interview is that the former is rarely seen or heard by anyone else, but there are exceptions. Some newspapers and magazines post audio or video clips on their websites; and, if an interview is recorded, if any contentious issues arise, a media lawyer will listen to decide whether the publication is vulnerable to being sued.

Some print interviewers rely less on their interviewing skills and more on research and writing to pull them through. A story that hinges on a seemingly dull, unquotable guest can be enlivened by diligent fact-gathering and lively prose.

It's possible to bluff your way through a broadcast interview, and rely on the guest to carry it, but there's no such luxury for a writer who sits down and begins to compose.

Some print reporters have never been taught how to interview nor do they get any feedback once they begin because their interviewing techniques are rarely heard by anyone else.

Thrown into a sink-or-swim situation, they usually don't drown, but they may not learn the most effortless or artistic ways of cutting through the waves. Bad habits can develop and may never be corrected.

"Most print journalists can't stand the way they interview," Roy MacGregor says. "If you ever filmed a print journalist interviewing, that person would probably be laughed right out of his work."

Print interviewers, in my opinion, need to bring the same kind of energy, presence, structure and conversational skills to interviews that most broadcasters automatically employ. Some do, of course; the requirement to add a video component to their reporting is perhaps forcing many to adopt the broadcast style.

RECORDING THE INTERVIEW

Some interviewers can take accurate notes and manage an interview at the same time, but most of us record the conversation.

Despite my aversion to transcribing (finding a reliable online service that quickly produces fairly accurate renditions at a reasonable cost is, to me, a godsend), I always use a recorder, if I can.

I do it for several reasons: my handwriting is atrocious; I want to have a copy of what was said, sometimes for legal reasons; and I find it challenging to scribble notes while listening attentively, observing body language, and thinking on my feet.

I doubt you could find a how-to book that endorses burying your face in a notebook while trying to communicate at your utmost level.

Once the formal part of the interview is about to begin (after trying to establish trust and rapport), I turn on my machine and say something like this: "I'm going to be taping our conversation because my magazine (or whoever I'm working for) wants to make sure that anything I quote is accurate. It's there to protect you." I then place it off to one side, rather than directly in front of the speaker, so they aren't watching it record.

ZOOM INTERVIEWS

I've found the Zoom audio often breaks up and some of what the interviewee says is lost.

For a book project in late 2021, I asked that we switch from Zoom interviews to telephone conversations for that very reason.

I had no technical problems with the latter.

I also say I'll be checking from time to time to ensure the recorder is still working. I strongly encourage this because machines do malfunction, usually for a technical reason, such as dead batteries. I started saying this when I noticed some interviewees becoming concerned when I looked at the recorder and they actually stopped talking to ask if everything was all right. By informing them in advance, I find few do this.

If the person objects to being taped, I'll take a quiet but assertive stance, saying a camera has to be used for a TV interview and the tape recorder is my version of that. I try to use a tone that suggests the matter isn't negotiable.

If that doesn't work, I'll propose the following: "Why don't we start and see how it goes. If at any time you're not comfortable, we can stop." At that point I'll turn on the recorder and start the interview. This almost always works.

As I record, I also take notes, which I highly recommend. Most of the time, I use the notebook to jot down reminders of areas to bring up or return to during the interview. I also write down my observations about the interviewee (dress, posture, habits, etc.) and anything pertinent in the space where the interview is taking place. These descriptions are often included in the story.

LASTING LONGER

In general, print interviews (especially for feature stories) take longer than those for broadcast. To tell a story accurately and thoroughly, the print interviewer typically needs to elicit a large amount of detail and description, especially when reconstructing events. A broadcast interviewer primarily mines for compelling anecdotes and displays of emotion.

A broadcaster can have a guest say, "When I was a young boy, something amazing happened to me," and then have the guest tell an anecdote. A print interviewer needs to know where and when exactly it occurred, at what age, family details, why it happened and likely many more specifics. An engaging anecdote won't stand alone.

At this point in my career, most of my interviews are for books. They can cover a lot of ground, and often last up to two hours. I find that going longer is counterproductive, as both the guest and I are exhausted by then.

Unlike for broadcast, a print interview can start slowly, although time management is still the interviewer's responsibility. I always ask how much time the person has for the interview and if it's shorter than I had hoped for, I'll say: "Is that a hard deadline? Do I need to be finished by that time or is there any leeway?"

Unless there's an absolute deadline, I find—as I believe most interviewers do—that a person who's engaged in the conversation doesn't notice how much time has passed, or they don't care.

Most of my print interviews begin the same way:

- I confirm the spelling of the person's first and last name. Never assume either. (I have a friend who spells his first name Tedd, not Ted.) I do this even if I have their business card as I want to have the correct information on the transcribed version of the interview.
- If they have a name such as Robert or Katherine, I ask whether they prefer I use their full name or a shorter version (Bob, Kate).
- Their age.
- Where they were born.
- Their title (if applicable).
- Any other background questions I need for my story.

As I pose these questions, I closely observe the interviewee for signs of undue nervousness, how they speak (spontaneously or measured?), and perhaps their attitude towards the process. These observations help me decide how I'll manage the interview.

During the interview, I try to read the interviewee's energy level, especially if a fair amount of time has passed. If it seems to be waning, I'll say: "We've been talking for a while, so I'm just checking in for a moment to see how you're doing."

I won't do this if there's critical information I still need. Stopping for a breather could result in the person asking to end the interview, which could backfire for, say, an accountability interview.

At the end, I turn off my machine and thank the interviewee. Once the official interview has ended, a person often adds critical information that I'll need for the story, perhaps as we walk to the door or an elevator.

That's why I always carry my recorder in one hand, ready to be turned on again right away. If something comes up, I might say, "That was really interesting. Do you think you could repeat it for me on tape?" Most of the time they'll comply.

WHEN WRITING OR RECORDING ISN'T POSSIBLE

You can't always use a recorder, for a variety of reasons. On one occasion, for a Toronto Life *magazine article, I was allowed to attend a birthday party for a member of a family of four I was writing about. Using a notebook or recorder during that event would have been intrusive.*

So I did what many writers do in such circumstances: I made a few trips to the washroom, where I wrote down notes. Later, when I was alone in my car and on the way home, I dictated everything I could remember into my recorder.

In no-recording-allowed circumstances, try to burn important quotes into your memory, perhaps by repeating them to yourself, over and over. Then find the fastest way to write them down or record them.

WHAT THEY HAVE A RIGHT TO KNOW

It never ceases to amaze me how often the interviewee doesn't know or is unclear about what's going on. If there's any doubt—for example, if someone else arranged the interview—I typically say the following: "I just want to confirm that you know who I am, who I'm working for and what the interview is about."

Occasionally, I add some other information, such as the length of the article/broadcast, when it will appear, my focus, who else I'm talking to for the piece, and what I hope to achieve in our conversation.

I might mention that examples help to make a story more compelling. I always prefer them to be on the record, but occasionally I agree to disguise them (many professionals fear violating confidentiality, so this might encourage them to share some stories they'd otherwise suppress), as long as the lack of an identified source isn't an ethical concern.

If we both know there are contentious things to discuss, I might comment that: "I'm sure you're aware that I'm going to be asking you about X." I say it in a matter-of-fact tone, as another way of letting them I'm there to do my job in an open and not underhanded manner.

I believe interviewees have a right to know any and all of this information (with few exceptions, such as in high-risk undercover assignments). In fact, if they're media-trained, as many are, they might ask for this information before agreeing to start the interview.

When I lay out my cards, unprompted, it tends to help create a greater level of trust between us.

KEY TAKEAWAYS

- Apply all interviewing techniques to a print interview, including the need for a dynamic.
- It's more than appropriate to start off by asking basic background questions.
- Unless there's a legitimate reason, tell the interviewee as much about what you're up to as possible; it makes them calmer and, usually, more cooperative.

THIRTY-SIX: **TELEPHONE AND EMAIL INTERVIEWS**

The vast majority of interviews I've conducted over the decades have been on the telephone, not face-to-face. I'd wager that's the same for many, if not most, journalists, including those who work in radio. Now, some interviews take place over Zoom, Skype, or another form of videotelephony, as this technology is called. Although they have a visual element, I consider them a variation on the telephone interview.

When lecturing on interviewing, I'm invariably asked to explain the difference between an in-person interview and one that's done over the phone. My answer is always the same: one is done in person and the other on the phone, except in the latter you can't see the other person or their surroundings.

That's it, or it should be.

Unfortunately, that's not how it always plays out. Too many interviewers treat the telephone interview far too casually.

Most of the time for in-person encounters, we're in the person's territory, such as their office or home, or at an event where the interviewee is participating in something noteworthy. We're generally aware of how we look, dress, sit, and otherwise comport ourselves.

For telephone interviews, because there's no visual

scrutiny, some interviewers forget many of the basic interviewing principles.

The most serious mistake is distraction. With the opportunity to access their computer and smartphone as the interviewee talks (and relying on a recording device to do the listening), some interviewers can't resist checking their devices.

As for listening, as noted earlier, a recording device can become a crutch during an interview, allowing the questioner to drift off. When that happens, people can often tell you're not listening, even if they can't see you. "Are you still there?" they'll ask, indicating they don't feel your presence on the other end of the line.

Veteran journalist Peter Desbarats said he was often interviewed after he chaired a Royal Commission on the concentration of ownership and control of newspapers in Canada. "You can tell rapidly if somebody's just doing it [interviewing] because it's a job, or if he's made up his mind beforehand what you're going to say. Even on the telephone, you get that kind of bored feedback coming back and it really turns you off."

Sloppy posture and other lazy body language actions also are a hazard for phone interviews. I position myself in a comfortable but assertive manner before placing the call. It affects how I perform, helping me be more alert. Some (many?) telephone interviewers don't even consider this factor. They slouch or fidget or otherwise don't think about how they should be presenting themselves physically, as if it has no bearing on how they come across.

A telephone interview eliminates many physical imbalances between you and the guest (although many people will do an image search to get a sense of your appearance). It also allows you to have detailed notes and lists of questions in front of you.

The telephone can be a wonderful resource for an interviewer; just treat it with the respect it deserves and not as one more phone call. Make a telephone conversation as special as a face-to-face interview.

DON'T DIAL TOO SOON

A common mistake is to pick up the phone too soon. Prepare for the phone interview the way you would for one in person, including how you will present yourself to the interviewee. Identify yourself, which entity you're representing, and what story you're working on. Explain why you're calling.

Because many people have been media-trained, they've been taught to ask questions before agreeing to an interview, such as: What's your focus? How long is your story? Who else are you talking to? How much time will you need? What's your deadline? Do you have any examples of your work you could send me?

If you can't answer these questions, don't place the call yet.

During the interview, try to prompt the interviewee to paint pictures of anything you would like described. Not everyone is good at doing that, however, so don't become impatient with a person who can't provide the level of description you need.

If the person isn't visually dominant, try switching to another sense, such as auditory, smell, or kinesthetic: Do you remember any important conversations you had at the time? Do you recall what the house/room smelled like? Can you grasp what the person was trying to say?

For a *Canadian Medical Association Journal* article on doctors who'd served in Afghanistan, my first interviewee struggled to describe in detail a hospital that had been constructed in what amounted to the middle of a desert. He had a clear auditory memory but was not good at providing a visual picture.

However, the next doctor I interviewed was the opposite. He could walk me through every nook and cranny of the building. Both were extremely cooperative, but with different dominances.

THE VOICE CAN SAY A LOT

In December 2020, during the pandemic, Hadley Freeman, a writer for The Guardian, *wrote about why she enjoyed conducting interviews over the telephone:*

"They've been great. Interviewing is all about listening and doing them from a distance has made me focus on that instead of getting distracted by the externals.

"Describing fashion editor André Leon Talley's rather extraordinary way of speaking—all courtly southern manners with European accents—probably conveyed his personality at least as well as describing his similarly extraordinary physical appearance would have done.

"Talking to [actor] Geena Davis by phone late at night, her in her bed in LA, me in mine in London, gave our encounter an intimacy I can't imagine we'd have managed had we met in person."

THE EMAIL INTERVIEW

If my students are any sample, many of today's journalists would rather email questions than talk to a person directly or over the phone.

Sending questions by email is an easy way to harvest quotes, but it's not an interview. It can also be a burden for the recipient. Students often send me emails with questions that would require a major investment of my time to answer. I usually say they have to phone me instead.

Bear this in mind when deciding whether email is the best method to accomplish your goals.

It can be a quick and efficient way to gather information or quotes for a story, but there's little opportunity to challenge or deconstruct or explore a response. That can be done in follow-up questions, but by using email, the interviewer loses control.

If you must use email to ask questions, there are a few points to keep in mind:

- Your initial subject line is important. As noted earlier, I use "Media Interview Request."
- Clearly and concisely explain what you're working on.
- Your questions must make sense and be easy to answer.
- Ask one question at a time. I often send them as a numbered list, not in paragraph form, to ensure they're all addressed.
- If possible, encourage the person to offer details and anecdotes.
- Mention your deadline.

KEY TAKEAWAYS

- A common mistake is to pick up the phone too soon.
- Treat a telephone interview the same way you would one conducted in person.
- The subject line is the most important part of an email interview request.

THIRTY-SEVEN: **STREETERS**

One year, when I worked at CBC Radio's morning program in Ottawa, my primary job was to gather comments on the street from average citizens about topics of interest in the news, or at public events, asking for their reactions to what had just transpired. I quickly learned what worked in these often-awkward situations and what didn't.

Streeters, as we called them, are harder to do than they might seem. It's not just a matter of shoving a microphone in someone's face and posing questions. First, you have to persuade them to stop and talk to you, which is easier to accomplish if you have a TV cameraperson with you, especially if you're out on the street. The camera does tend to entice people; less so a radio mike or a notebook.

I would move towards them, often stepping into their way, although not aggressively, and introduce myself: "Hi, I'm sorry to bother you. My name is Paul McLaughlin, I work for the morning CBC Radio program and I'm here to ask people a few questions about X."

I could usually tell within a few seconds whether the person was a potential interviewee, often just by their body language.

Some people declined my invitation, fearing they'd sound inarticulate. "Don't worry about that," I'd say. "I'll edit this and make us both sound good!" That often worked.

I'd preface my question with information that might help them come up with a response.

For example, if I was gathering comments about a federal budget, instead of, "What do you think of the budget?" I'd ask something like this: "The new federal budget said almost nothing about what the government would do about equal pay for women. What do you think about that?"

Depending on the answer, I'd explore the reasons for their opinion. The best clips came after my initial question, and my best follow-up question was this: "Why do you think that way?" I'd spend several minutes with someone I thought was an interesting speaker, delving into the reasons for their opinions.

I've seen journalists conduct streeters as a one-question exercise. The end result was a predictable response that offered little or no insight.

I took a positive attitude with me on these assignments because I believed people were interesting and had something worthwhile to say. Although that didn't always turn out to be true, I treated all of them with respect.

Interestingly, the more I assumed they had something to say, the more often I came back to the studio with something of value.

KEY TAKEAWAY

- For streeters, give people a specific, rather than a general, question to consider.

THIRTY-EIGHT: **DIFFICULT INTERVIEWS**

Although most interviews progress in a civil manner, there are exceptions. A famous encounter took place in April 2009 between then-CBC Radio host Jian Ghomeshi (more on him later) and actor/musician Billy Bob Thornton.

Ghomeshi's national program, _Q_, which also was broadcast on YouTube, and throughout North America on radio, invited The Boxmasters, an eclectic rock'n'roll group founded in 2007, onto the program for a live chat. (Transparency: I trained Ghomeshi just before he took over as the host of _Q_.) The band, fronted by Hollywood star Billy Bob Thornton, had come to Toronto, where _Q_ was produced, to open for country stars Willie Nelson and Ray Price.

Ghomeshi began with a fairly long introduction that noted the band's accomplishments. He then mentioned that its singer and drummer "is a guy named Billy Bob Thornton whose other job, some of the time, is Oscar-winning screenwriter, actor, director. [But] The Boxmasters is anything but a diversion from the silver screen. He's always intended to make music..."

As Ghomeshi completed his intro, the YouTube audience could see Thornton, to the host's left, scowling. Ghomeshi asked his first question:

JG: "Billy Bob, you guys formed in only the last couple of years, right?"

BBT: "I don't know what you're talking about."

Ghomeshi laughed nervously.

JG: "How so?"

BBT: "I don't know what you mean by that."

JG: "When did the band form?"

BBT: "I'm not sure."

The other band members, all of whom looked extremely uncomfortable, then offered some answers. About the 2:30 mark, Ghomeshi tried with Thornton again.

JG: "What have you learned from Willie Nelson?"

BBT: "Never met him," which was obviously untrue as they were touring together.

Thornton's answers became increasingly bizarre, until he finally divulged the problem: one of the show's producers had agreed, he alleged, that there would not be a single reference of any kind to Thornton's film work during the interview. It was a condition, he said, that Ghomeshi broke in the introduction.

The host, who had been a musician of some limited success in Canada, tried to explain that it was "context" to include the biographical information. After some more uncomfortable back and forth, Ghomeshi asked:

"Do you want to continue if we talk about music?"

"That would be great," Thornton said, unenthusiastically.

Thornton finally answered some questions, but most of the allotted time for the interview had expired. After a few minutes, it was time for the band to play a number; Thornton refused to join them.

Ghomeshi's star was on the rise before the Thornton debacle, but afterwards it skyrocketed. Most observers applauded how he never lost his cool while they found Thornton's behavior—and his "no mention of my film career" requirement—idiotic.

While the interview is a classic illustration of how to remain cool and collected when dealing with a difficult guest, Ghomeshi's career demonstrates how easily a ride to the top can be followed by a plummet to the bottom.

Following the Thornton *cause célèbre*, the radio host became a North American star, who interviewed some of the biggest names in the arts—Leonard Cohen, Paul McCartney, Margaret Atwood, Joni Mitchell, and Barbra Streisand.

But in late 2014, his world collapsed, when the police charged him with sexual assault and choking, in what Ghomeshi had excused as consensual, rough-sex relationships.

The man who had seemed so seductive on radio was exposed as a dangerous predator, a "bad date," as some women wrote online. His rapid fall from grace made it clear that, in today's world, it's incredibly difficult for a prominent public figure to hide a dark side. (He was acquitted by a judge of the charges in March 2016. But the damage to his reputation, in Canada at least, was irreparable).

QUIET RESOLVE

I have a saying I very much believe in, although there can be exceptions to it (aren't there always?): "The harder the question, the softer the voice." By this I mean that usually it's unwise to ask a difficult question in a sharp or otherwise aggressive tone.

Few of us have been trained in confronting someone in person or over a phone or video link. As a result, I've seen examples of journalists acting in what can only be described as a pseudo-aggressive manner when the opposite tack should have been taken.

In a 1985 NBC documentary, *Portrait of the Press, Warts and All*, which examined the coverage of the murder of a middle-aged woman that took place near Seattle, a reporter came out to the trailer home of the woman's grieving daughter.

"First came the murder, then came the media," the daughter recalled. She said a reporter wedged his foot in her front door and tried to force his way in, badly bruising her shoulder in the struggle. "He yelled at me, 'What's the matter with you, lady, I didn't murder anyone!'"

That's an egregious example, but there are countless others where the interviewer's nervousness, inexperience, or just downright insensitivity emerges.

Most of the time, I encourage interviewers to pose a challenging question—for example, in an interview with a politician who voted for city hall to develop a parcel of land, "Do you own the numbered company that owns the land you voted to purchase at the last city hall meeting?"—in the same tone you'd use to ask if the person wanted a cup of coffee.

Occasionally, you need to be more aggressive in your tone, especially if the person is yelling at you. It's not normal, or recommended, that you respond in a namby-pamby voice in a situation that calls for a more heated response. Doing so can infuriate an angry person even more.

Here's a technique I've found works. It was suggested to me by former RCMP interviewing specialist Frank

Byrnes. If the other person yells at you, meet their tone in your first response. After that, keep reducing your tone down, as if you were slowly turning down a radio dial, until you get to what you consider to be a normal voice. When I've tried this, I've had considerable success with it.

DEALING WITH APPALLING VIEWPOINTS

Your job is to reveal, rather than to judge or condemn. Resist the temptation, especially in a broadcast interview, to show the audience that you don't subscribe to whatever seemingly foul notion an interviewee might be spewing. If the person says something racist or hateful, for example, you can indicate that you don't agree with what they said, but you don't need to belabor your reaction to ensure, in your mind, that the audience (if it's recorded) knows you don't subscribe to such views.

How you react to an egregious comment by a guest, however, can be a tricky and delicate challenge.

An artful example took place in October 1964, in the first month of the iconic CBC TV investigative program *This Hour Has Seven Days* (which paved the way for programs such as *60 Minutes*), when it brought George Lincoln Rockwell, the self-styled commander of the American Nazi party, into the studio. He was a smug individual who wore Nazi regalia and smoked a corncob pipe throughout the exchange with two of the program's questioners, Douglas Leiterman and Robert Hoyt.

Rockwell espoused views about Jews and African Americans (he didn't use that wording) that would have made it impossible to air the interview on network television today. At one point, when discussing Black people, Rockwell said, "You people in Canada, I don't think you have any [derogatory word] running around up there, do you?"

Leiterman breathed out nervously, then decided to answer. "Well Commander, I wouldn't like to go into a description of what you might describe as a [derogatory word] unless you'd like to," he said.

Rockwell took the bait and barreled ahead with more despicable comments. It was a wonderful illustration of the (sometimes) effectiveness of throwing a question posed by an interviewee back at them. Rockwell seemed to revel in attention and likely had no interest in what Leiterman might say.

A few moments later, after Rockwell proffered another negative depiction of African Americans, Leiterman again stepped in, in a quiet, controlled voice: "Commander, that's not a very good description of the Negroes we have in Canada," he said, using a word that was acceptable in 1964.

It was an impressive example of how to show restraint with a guest whose views are repulsive. By not fighting with Rockwell (who was murdered by a former member of his fledgling party some three years later), the interviewers allowed him to expose his vile beliefs.

Robert MacNeil exhorted interviewers not to regard the process as an intrinsically hostile affair. "Part of my approach is that this is not a prosecutorial situation," he said. "We're not here to embarrass people and make them look bad. We're here to elicit information and get them to share their views and knowledge with us and the people listening.

"The prosecutorial style is largely empty and theatrical, but it makes the interviewer look very tough and it directs a lot of attention toward him. This approach only contributes to the perception of arrogance and condescension in the media, perceptions, which I'm afraid, have a basis in fact."

Eric Malling, a relentless, aggressive TV interviewer, also decried the need to flex his muscles unnecessarily: "I get them to tell their side of the story. I think they should be prepared to be consistent and if they start saying things that aren't true and I have information otherwise, I'm going to point it out as forcefully as is required. But I don't beat anybody up and never have. And even if I wanted to, I wouldn't get away with it because the sympathy of the audience immediately goes to the person on the other side."

FIND A WAY IN

Some people are known to be unpleasant to journalists and, as a consequence, many reporters either avoid talking to them, or approach them so timidly they lose confidence and fail to get what they need.

No matter how intimidating a potential interviewee might appear, there just might be a way to forge a connection, especially if you can find a way that's not related to the business at hand.

That's the approach Gerald Eskenazi, veteran *New York Times* writer and author of numerous books, said he took when asked to get a quote from a notoriously difficult baseball player.

"The Boston Red Sox had a star named Jim Rice, the bane of sportswriters. He hated us. But the paper wanted me to get his take on a teammate, Fred Lynn, who was having a great year," Eskenazi wrote in "The Art of the Tough Interview," published in the *Columbia Journalism Review* in 2015. "'Jim Rice?' said a Boston writer. 'Good luck. He won't talk to you. He never talks to the press.'

"Well, I went to his locker before a game. I introduced myself and held out my hand. He let it stay there, frozen. 'Now what?' I thought. And then I remembered: My nine-year-old son Mark had a Jim Rice-model glove. It was a year old, but I lied a little.

"'Jim,' I said, as he ignored me and put on his uniform, 'I just got my son a Jim Rice glove, and I don't know how to break it in. The leather is very stiff.'

"He stopped dressing. He reached into the top shelf of his locker and pulled out a glove. 'Here's what you do,' he began, and launched into a nonstop explanation: How you oil it, how you put a ball inside the glove and then tie it all together to mold the glove's shape. I couldn't stop him from talking.

"'Anything else?' he asked, pleasantly.

"'Yeah, I'm doing a story on Fred Lynn,' I said.

"'Oh—a picture out of *Vogue*, the way he swings the bat,' said Rice, my pal. Thanks for that great quote, Jim. It made my second paragraph."

IF THE INTERVIEW BECOMES PROBLEMATIC

I've talked to many interviewers who told me, after the fact, that an interview didn't work, that they left feeling something was wrong. But they didn't deal with it during the conversation.

If an interview doesn't seem to be going well, especially if I think the interviewee is upset or annoyed, I'll employ an extremely aggressive tactic—I'll speak the truth (from my perspective).

For a print interview, I'll use wording such as this: "I'm just going to pause for a moment because I'm sensing that you're upset about something. I wonder whether I've said something you're not happy with." I say this in a quiet but assertive tone, not accusatory.

It's deliberate to suggest the fault (if there is one) is mine. For one thing, it could be true. For another, it lessens the aggressiveness of my challenge.

I only revert to this kind of direct confrontation when I believe a) that nothing else is working, and b) I don't have all the information I need for my story. If you have nothing to lose, and conduct yourself in a polite and professional manner, why not try to lance the boil, so to speak, while you're still there? Especially for a print interview, it's worth a shot.

I might also use this approach for a taped broadcast interview, knowing the exchange could be included in the end product. For a live broadcast interview, I probably wouldn't pause the interview, but would look for a playful way to respond to the interviewee's apparent discomfort.

"Did that question bother you?" I might say in a light-hearted tone, or "Are you okay with these questions?" Bear in mind that a guest might snap back. "What do you mean? I'm fine." A response such as that requires you to either say, "Okay. Just checking," and continue with your questions, or, "I just got the feeling that you weren't happy with what I've been asking," or other words to that effect.

NECKLACE AND HEELS

In 1986, when Linda MacLennan was co-anchoring Canada AM, the CTV network's national morning show based in Toronto, she was assigned to interview one of the most intimidating politicians of the day—Margaret Thatcher.

As part of her preparation, MacLennan, who stands about 5'7", "wore the highest heels I owned," to boost her physical presence compared to the Conservative British prime minister, who was about 5'4". Here's how MacLennan describes the experience:

"[It was] at the height of the Commonwealth crisis about sanctions against South Africa. I flew to London for an interview with the Iron Lady [as she was called]. She was the only Commonwealth leader opposed to sanctions. The interview was in her private quarters at 10 Downing Street. I was so nervous—it was Thatcher. It was on her turf. And I knew that at least part of the interview would be contentious.

"I got there early so I could just sit, get comfortable and not let the surroundings intimidate me. Then she strode into the room, we shook hands and got right down to business. When I questioned her position in the face of worldwide calls for sanctions against apartheid, she clearly didn't like it. She leaned forward in her chair and tried to turn the tables, challenging me with her own question and hoping to show that I didn't know what I was talking about.

> "'Do you know what the necklace is?' she asked, referring to a barbaric practice used by some members of the Black community to punish those whom they believed to be collaborating with the apartheid government. Necklacing involved igniting a rubber tire filled with gasoline that had been forced over a victim's chest and arms. It was a slow and horrific way to die. "I did [know what it was], thank God."
>
> MacLennan also had a moment of triumph: "There's a great photo of us shaking hands, and I'm towering over her. Tiny victories!"

ONE-MINUTE ANSWERS

Covering professional athletes is not always easy. I was once told this story about a member of the Toronto Blue Jays who ended up in baseball's Hall of Fame.

A reporter would cautiously approach him and ask if he had a minute to talk. The player would say sure but after exactly one minute of saying nothing of substance he'd walk away. He did this a lot.

There are countless other examples of athletes being difficult to deal with.

One journalist who has found a way to communicate with most of them is Shi Davidi, who offers these strategies for dealing with athletes:

- "Keep in mind that you're entering their office, their workspace, their day. It's important to be respectful and gracious and understanding.

- *"I'm big on starting light. Warm up the person. Maybe ask, 'How did you feel tonight went?' It's a good, generic question. If you can get a sense of where the athlete thinks his performance was, then you can build off that.*
- *"When guys see that you work hard, they generally respect that. They're grinding so hard every day and if they see you're doing the same they [notice] that. But if they see you parachuting in, and taking a few jabs and then parachuting out, they have less time for you."*

KEY TAKEAWAYS

- Don't fight a really belligerent interviewee. Try to find out why they're so upset.
- You don't need to prove that you disagree with an interviewee's objectionable comments. Your questions can make that clear.
- Your best defense in a difficult interview is being really well-informed.

THIRTY-NINE: **DON'T APOLOGIZE FOR A QUESTION**

It's as simple as this: if you believe a question is worth asking, just ask it.

Over the years, I've heard many variations of the following:

- You probably don't want to answer this, but...
- Maybe I shouldn't be asking you this...
- This is probably too personal but...
- Maybe it's none of my business...

These preambles betray nervousness and uncertainty, and that is not a positive way to begin a difficult or sensitive question. There's nothing to be gained by doing it, and there is something to lose—the interviewee could throw your wording back at you, to avoid the question.

Q: This is probably too personal but...

A: You're right. It is too personal. Next question.

Ask the question in a normal voice, and in a polite manner, without apologizing for it. Even if the interviewee chooses not to answer, the way they avoid it will be revealing.

KEY TAKEAWAY

- Never apologize for asking a question.

FORTY: **WHAT IF THEY QUESTION ME?**

In 1975, British TV talk show host Michael Parkinson awkwardly opened an interview with actor Helen Mirren, age 30 at the time, with: "I mean, you are, in quotes, a serious actress."

"What do you mean 'in quotes?'"

Parkinson stumbled through a feeble response, then bridged to where he was intending to go: "Do you find that this—what could be best described as your equipment—in fact, hinders you, perhaps, in that pursuit?"

"I'd like you to explain what you mean by my 'equipment,' in great detail."

"I think they might sort of detract from the performance, if you know what I mean," he said.

"Because serious actresses can't have big bosoms, is that what you mean?" she asked. "I can't think that could necessarily be true. I mean, what a crummy performance if people are obsessed with the size of your bosom or anything else. I would hope that the performance and the [stage] play, and the living relationship between all the people on stage, and all the people in the audience would overcome such boring questions, really."

This infamous exchange illustrates what can happen when the interviewer takes the conversation down a path that invites the guest to challenge his question.

In doing so, Mirren revealed the 40-year-old Parkinson to be, certainly on this occasion, a boorish fool.

The tables can be turned on you at any time. You might ask what you believe to be a reasonable question, only to have it thrown back at you, with the interviewee demanding you explain what you mean.

It's not uncommon for an interviewee to answer a question with a question. In my experience, if you say nothing in response, most people will keep talking.

But sometimes, the return question must be answered. Can you anticipate this? Well, yes, to a degree.

If you're about to discuss a controversial topic—such as abortion or capital punishment—your prep should include the possibility the guest will ask where you stand on the issue.

Whether you answer is up to you. But you need to plan what you'll say. As an example, if I were asked the abortion question, I wouldn't lie. I'd say that I support a woman's choice to have an abortion, but think it would not be an easy decision for anyone involved. I'd say it calmly and without any indication that I wanted to fight about the topic.

Then I'd bridge, "But no one is interested in my opinion. We're here to learn what you believe, what you think, so I'd love to hear your thoughts on abortion."

In most cases, silence will chase the question away; or repeating the question; or you may simply want to say, "It doesn't matter what I think."

Whether or not to respond is a case-by-case decision but try not to engage in a debate with an interviewee. You might come out on top, but many of the people we interview are skilled speakers. That's often why they were selected for an interview.

Our job, our role, is to ask the questions. If you keep this in mind (understanding there are exceptions), then the interchange between you and the guest should flow from this awareness.

KEY TAKEAWAYS

- Try not to answer questions directed at you; but sometimes you must.
- Often, by remaining silent when asked a question, the interviewee will jump back in without you having to say anything.
- Try to anticipate if the story you're working on could lead to an interviewee challenging you on your perspective.

FORTY-ONE: **INTERVIEWING VICTIMS**

In the early 1980s, in preparation for a series of articles to run on Victoria Day weekend, a time in Canada when traffic fatalities are traditionally high, Don Gibb, a reporter with the *London Free Press*, received an assignment many journalists dread—interview a family member who lost a loved one in a car accident on a previous Victoria Day weekend.

The ill feeling emerges from not knowing what kind of response you'll receive. Some people might welcome you into their homes; others might accuse you of being ghoulish, exploitive of their grief and only interested in selling newspapers (or TV commercials or amassing clicks…). Some can be verbally abusive and even threaten physical harm.

(Many years ago, a friend told me that after one of his brothers died in a snowmobile accident on a lake, his other brother, who was a cop, told a local TV reporter that if he took any film of the body being recovered, he would out him as a gay man. This was at a time when that could have been devastating for the reporter's career. The reporter didn't use any visuals for his story.)

There can also be a personal anguish for the reporter, a feeling that you're either intruding on someone's raw emotions (if the interview comes immediately or soon after the tragedy) or, in the case of "anniversary" stories such as Gibb's, reopening painful old wounds.

Gibb, who became a journalism professor at Ryerson University (now Toronto Metropolitan University) and a writing coach after ending a 20-year career at the *Press*, phoned a man whose 21-year-old son had been killed in a motorcycle crash the previous year. Despite having done an estimated 50 of these types of interactions before, Gibb, who has a warm and friendly demeanor, was nervous nonetheless about what reaction he might get.

When he arrived at the man's door, he held in his hand a copy of the story the *Press* ran when the accident occurred. "It was a mere four paragraphs or so that was awfully sterile and based only on information provided by police," he says.

When the father saw the clipping, he said it was a terrible story. And then he asked: "Why didn't a reporter call me [at the time]?"

"Would you have talked to a reporter?"

"I don't know," the man replied, "but I would have liked the call."

Gibb says he learned a valuable lesson that day, one he shared with his journalism students over the years. "[After that] I approached the task with a better understanding of what was important. Those who had lost someone deserved the right to speak just as much as they deserved the right to say no. We were denying them this right because many reporters considered it an invasion of privacy. My response is this: it's not an invasion of privacy unless, or until, they tell me it is."

From that point on, Gibb would say the following to someone he contacted to ask for an interview about the loss of a loved one: "Hi, my name is Don Gibb and I'm writing a story for the paper about the death of your daughter. I thought I owed it to you to give you a chance to tell us about her."

It made the task much easier because Gibb knew exactly why he was doing it. "They had a right [to talk to me] and I was going to honor it rather than simply rely on the starkness of a police report."

RESPECT THE VICTIMS

Early one afternoon in 2007, in my role as off-camera interviewer for *Fraud Squad TV*, my crew and I met a young couple, likely in their early 30s, in Jacksonville, Florida. Their two young children (both under age eight) had died of carbon monoxide poisoning in a fire. A shoddily made (counterfeit) disco ball they'd won at a children's game room that day caused it.

That evening, after the mother had tucked them in and turned out the lights in the room they shared, the children plugged in the ball and played with it under a cover. The ball had a lightbulb inside it that rotated and threw off strobe lights.

If, for any reason, the plastic side of the ball came into contact with the bulb, a properly made disco ball would automatically shut down. The counterfeit ball did not have that safety feature. By the time the mother realized a fire had broken out in their bedroom, it was too late to save her children.

Their lawyers, who had initiated a lawsuit concerning the counterfeit product, connected us with the parents. Like many couples who lose a child, they had separated after the tragedy, but both came to their lawyers' office (the mother wore a t-shirt with pictures of the children on the front) to tell us what had happened. They were articulate, kind and spoke from a deep, dark place I hope never to visit.

We'd been at the law office on another story when this one was offered to us. Consequently, I had little time to prepare, although I felt confident all I would need to do was ask them what had happened.

I couldn't see my two fellow crew members, so I don't know whether they teared up as much as I did as the story unfolded. It was an emotionally shattering interview. Afterwards, as we were ready to leave, the mother pulled a thick cache of photographs from her purse. "These are pictures of our children," she said. "Would you like to see them?"

All three of us said yes, despite knowing it would not be an easy or brief experience. How could we say no after they had so generously poured their hearts out for our TV segment?

Sometimes you just can't stay because you have an unmovable deadline to meet, but we didn't have that excuse and, even if we had, we wouldn't have played it. By the time we'd seen all the pictures, we cancelled what was planned for the rest of the day and went for a much-needed drink instead.

TERMINOLOGY

The term 'victim' is preferred and is standard in its use within the criminal justice system. Note that some people who have been assaulted prefer to describe themselves as 'survivors' rather than victims.

AFTER THE INTERVIEW

Too often in journalism, we come into peoples' lives, grab our quotes or clips or whatever else we need to get the job done, then disappear, often without a thought about what we've left in our wake.

I remember, years ago, when I was a chase producer for CBC Radio, I pursued a man for some time, flattering and coaxing him to come on air. He later told me it was like being seduced, then dumped as soon as the sex was over.

"I'm interviewed a lot," he said, "and that's what it feels like. And I know lots of women who do interviews who agree. You hound us until we say yes and then, when it's over, you're gone. I've been live in a studio for, say, a five-minute chat, which goes by in a heartbeat, and then walked out of the studio and, at most, am handed over to someone to escort me to the door. Lots of times I'm literally left on my own. There's no cuddling."

I've never forgotten what he said and have always tried to "cuddle" in some way after an interview, if possible.

RESOURCES TO HELP

Few, if any of us, have been trained how to react in the face of someone else's debilitating pain. When I was asked one year to talk about interviewing victims of crime, which usually means surviving family members and friends, at the annual conference of the Canadian Association of Journalists, I decided to contact experts for advice.

"When there's a shooting at a school, I can't believe that the media constantly talks about 'bringing in grief counselors,' a member of the Canadian Resource Centre for the Victims of Crime told me. "Grief is a long-term process. Those kids are going through trauma. Use that word instead."

He also advised never to say, "I know what you're going through," or any other wording that suggests you understand what the loved ones of a victim are experiencing. "Unless you personally have lost a loved one to violence or an accident, much better to say, 'I can't imagine what you're going through.'"

About the same time as my CAJ presentation, a dear friend lost his 12-year-old son in a terrible accident and, naturally, was devastated. I asked the expert how to communicate with him. "A lot of people are afraid to even mention the name of the deceased out of fear that they'd upset the person," he said. "Don't do that. Not now or in the future. For example, don't be afraid to say, 'I bet your son would have loved that hockey game.' or whatever you know his son enjoyed. Don't make him disappear."

That was underlined for me when another friend, a lawyer, lost a teenage daughter, also in an accident. A year after her death, he and his wife (who had hardly left her bed during that time), decided to have a Hannukah party. At the end of the night, as they debriefed what had happened at the party, he said it felt like [their daughter] had been killed again. "No one mentioned her name," he said to me. This was not because they were bad people; quite the opposite. They thought that a mention of their daughter would be too upsetting for them.

I'm certain that journalists want to do and say the right thing when confronted with an interviewee who's in pain. The good news is that there are quite a few resources available to help us understand how to cover crime and its victims. The not-so-good news is that many (most?) journalists never access them.

An excellent guide for journalists is "Tips for Reporters when Working with Victims of Violent Crime," published in 2019 by Victims for Justice. I've edited the following for length:

- Approach the victim initially without equipment—notebooks, tape recorders, cameras, and lights—and try to make a human connection.
- Introduce yourself as a reporter, give the victim your name and title, and briefly explain what you hope to achieve.
- Express concern for the victim by saying, "I am sorry for what happened to you" or "I am sorry for your loss."
- Give the victim a reason to speak with you by explaining the purpose of the story, the fact that it will be published, and why the victim's participation is important.
- Clarify the ground rules—explain that anything the victim says may be used in the interview.
- Courteously accept the victim's refusal, if they are unwilling to be interviewed.
- If the victim declines, express interest in a future interview, leave a business card, or send an email with your contact information, and ask for the names of others who may be willing to speak.

Another significant resource is, "Reporting on Sexual Violence: A Guide for Journalists," a 2013 publication by the Minnesota Coalition Against Sexual Assault.

Its excellent advice includes a caveat to, "Avoid using the term 'alleged' rape or sexual assault. It reinforces the disbelief that a crime actually occurred. The term 'reported' is more neutral. It also indicates that a case is officially part of the justice system. But if the term 'alleged' is used, avoid labeling the victim as an 'accuser,' for this term also reinforces a negative stereotype.

By the way, there also are resources that instruct victims about us. For example, The Canadian Resource Centre for Victims of Crime has prepared *If the Media Calls: A Guide for Crime Victims & Survivors*.

MANY WANT TO TALK

In a 2012 article for the Canadian Association of Journalists, Don Gibb wrote about a New York Times *feature involving loved ones of victims of 9/11.*

"The collapse of the World Trade Center towers was about people who were loved, who had achievements and who had future goals," he observed. "The New York Times *wrote 200-word profiles on more than 2,400 individuals who died on Sept. 11, 2001. It's important to note that their families were willing to share their stories.*

"Titled 'Portraits of Grief,' Times *reporters spent more than a year compiling the profiles. Days after the attack, the profiles began filling one or more pages daily for four months. Not every family chose to talk and sometimes survivors of a victim could not be found. But of the roughly 2,800 people who died, 86 percent of their families willingly spoke to reporters. If families chose not to participate,* Times *reporters respected their wishes and did not go elsewhere to pursue a profile."*

A CALL FOR EMPATHY

"*Of the many human qualities required to be a great journalist—curiosity, carefulness, persistence, diligence, intelligence, integrity—it is empathy that ranks almost top of my list, second only to the curiosity that powers all great journalism,*" Kathy English wrote in a 2018 column in her role as public editor of The Toronto Star.

"*The empathetic journalist can imagine another's plight and pain, and in so doing, takes a critical step toward helping readers understand the plight and pain of another. The empathic journalist creates journalism that allows us to walk another's path, thus creating something more powerful than journalism—human connectedness.*"

KEY TAKEAWAYS

- Don't assume a victim or their family and friends don't want to talk.
- Never tell someone who has suffered a terrible loss that you know how they feel unless you've experienced a similar occurrence.
- Empathy is one of the most important characteristics for an interviewer.

FORTY-TWO: **INTERVIEWING MINORS**

I think the first child I interviewed was a young boy in Ottawa, about age seven, who had been appointed as an ambassador of a charity walkathon. It was for a short item on the CBC Radio morning show, so I only needed a few minutes of tape. I called his mother and she agreed to let me come to their home.

The three of us met in the family living room. I tried a variety of predictable questions, but his answers (perhaps because of my bland questions) seemed practiced and, frankly, unusable. He didn't sound like a seven-year-old.

I noticed that before each answer he looked at his mother, so I asked if she would be okay if I took her son outside to the backyard, without her, to see if a less formal setting would help. She kindly agreed.

Once outside, the boy, who was energetic and playful, pointed to a bee flying around in his garden. "That's Morris," he said. With that prompt, I asked him about Morris and about bees and about his interest in them. The result was a wonderful portrait of a seven-year-old, one that was far more interesting and authentic than what I had originally tried to get.

Interestingly, without knowing it of course, I was following one of the guidelines that later was recommended by the Education Writers Association (EWA) in their 2012 document, "Interviewing Children."

"If you are struggling to get a child talking, start by asking them about their hobbies and interests even if they aren't germane to the story."

The day I was introduced to Morris the bee, I realized how little I knew about interviewing children. Since then, I've come to understand a few things.

The first is that I need to anticipate what I can reasonably expect to get from a child, depending on their age. Too many journalists, I believe, either talk down to children, employing a condescending tone (a big mistake), or treat them as if they're adults and ask questions best suited for an older person.

So much depends on a child's age. There's a world of difference between, say, a nine-year-old and a fourteen-year-old.

In all cases involving a minor, an adult, such as a parent or teacher, should agree to the interview and be present when it takes place (no such requirement existed when I was a young interviewer).

Open-ended questions are almost a must, as a child can easily be led by an adult to agree to, or possibly corroborate, what the adult is saying.

I've found that group interviews sometimes work better than one-on-ones with children. Groups of young people talk excitedly among themselves, but when removed from the pack they often became reticent.

Consequently, for radio I liked to have a group talk among themselves, with my role predominantly relegated to being the person who held the microphone as they played off each other. Some young people, however, prefer one-on-ones. As usual, generalizations don't always apply.

Sadly, children are too often witnesses to violence

or trauma, be it at home, their neighborhood, or at school. Journalists should take "extreme caution when interviewing children" in cases such as this, the EWA says.

"In general, reporters should avoid doing this immediately after a tragedy. Instead, they should wait until the child is in a safe space with a parent or other trusted adult figure and has had time to process the event. They should realize that a child may still be in shock even if they do not outwardly exhibit signs of stress."

If you proceed with an interview, the EWA adds, "Reporters should make sure the child and parent understand where and when the interview will be broadcast or published. They should stop the interview immediately if the child becomes nervous, agitated, or frightened. Journalists who give families time and space to process and reflect on a traumatic event will generally end up with a much stronger and more complete story."

After the interview concludes, make sure an adult knows how to contact you, and provide pertinent information about where and when your story will appear. The EWA also suggests the following: "Journalists should be more lenient with children than adults when deciding whether to allow them to retract statements or review stories, manuscripts, and videos prior to publication.

"Most journalists would not allow a public official to alter or delete a controversial quote. But that practice is more acceptable with children, who are less media-savvy and may not immediately realize what's at stake when they agree to speak to the press."

If ever the "do no harm" principle applies, it's when minors are involved. No story is worth causing a child unnecessary trauma.

FEAR NOT THE CHILDREN

In the mid-1990s, Amanda Singroy, who was a reporter for CBC News at the time, covered a shooting in Toronto at which a five-year-old girl narrowly escaped being shot. Bullet holes riddled the hallway and kitchen of her home.

The next day, Singroy and two other TV journalists were allowed, by her mother, to interview the child.

"Myself and the CTV reporter asked questions such as 'What did you hear?' "Where was your mommy?' 'What did you do next?'" remembers Singroy.

A reporter for another network, however, "went a bit on the attack."

He asked, 'Were you/are you scared? Do you worry the people who had guns will come back?'"

Singroy and the other reporter intervened as soon as they heard him speaking to the child this way. "We pulled him aside and told him to lose the questions and we told the child not to answer. He was a junior reporter and [likely didn't realize] he was instilling fear into the child."

THE CJR'S ADVICE

The following is edited from a 2018 article by the Columbia Journalism Review entitled, "Conducting interviews with kids: do's and don'ts."

"Your tone, the type of questions you ask, and even your posture (don't talk down to kids, instead

kneel to their level) can have a negative impact on kids. Wherever possible, find a private, quiet place to conduct your interview.

"Do not interrogate them, and avoid jargon, using age-appropriate language. It's a good idea to offer a child breaks during long, difficult interviews; understand that they may tell a story of trauma or abuse to you out of chronological order.

"Don't put words in their mouths, and take extra care not to ask leading questions, especially to young, impressionable kids who might feel compelled to tell you what they think you want to hear.

"Social media can offer reporters easy access to kids when on deadline. Despite the fact that teenagers are so-called digital natives, don't assume that every child understands the public nature of their online behavior, and be sure to explain the consequences of their consent to an interview with you in an online setting, the same way you'd do in person.

KEY TAKEAWAYS

- If you're struggling to get a child talking, start by asking them about their hobbies and interests even if they aren't germane to the story.
- Sometimes children talk more readily if they are part of a group.
- Don't talk down to children or treat them like adults. Find the appropriate way to speak to them based on their age.

FORTY-THREE: **LONG PREAMBLES**

In the spring of 2020, I listened to a radio interview with veteran golf writer Michael Bamberger, who was promoting his new book, *The Second Life of Tiger Woods*.

Most authors on a book tour are incredibly kind and patient. They want to sell their book and see no benefit in upsetting an interviewer. Bamberger was no exception that day.

At one point the host asked a question that seemed to last almost two minutes. He summed up, in some detail, the major events that had happened in Tiger's life from the 2009 incident when Elin, his wife at the time, smashed his SUV with a golf club (this was prior to the terrible car accident of 2021). He listed the sex scandals that dominated the headlines in the following months, Tiger's numerous physical problems, the decline in his golf game for many years afterwards, and his incredible return to the top when he won the 2019 Masters tournament for a fifth time.

When the interviewer finally ended his preamble, he asked the writer for his thoughts on what he'd just said. "I think you summed it up very well," Bamberger replied, without even a hint of sarcasm.

Sometimes, detailed preambles are necessary, especially in broadcast interviews. They can save time by allowing you to provide a concise summation of information that might have taken much longer to extract from the interviewee. They also can help the interviewee—and sometimes the audience—understand where you're heading with your line of questioning.

Problems occur when the preamble is too long, unclear or—this is especially true of sports interviews—the interviewer is trying to show off how much they know about the topic or the sport in question.

Walter Koster, a journalist with the German newspaper *Saarbrücker Zeitung*, was notorious for asking long questions at Formula One news conferences, although his critics begrudgingly admitted they were often insightful.

In November 2014, Koster addressed a panel of six drivers at a presser for the Abu Dhabi Grand Prix in his slow, halting English. "Gentlemen, a short view back to the past. Thirty years ago, Niki Lauda told us, 'Take a monkey, place him into the cockpit and he is able to drive the car.'

"Thirty years later Sebastian [Vettel, who was on the panel] told us I had to start my car like a computer. It's very complicated. And Nico Rosberg [who was also on the panel] said that during the race, I don't really remember what race, he pressed the wrong button on the wheel.

"Question for you both: Is Formula One driving today too complicated with twenty and more buttons on the wheel? Are you too much under effort, under pressure? What are your wishes for the future concerning the technical program during the race? Less buttons? More? Or less or more communication with your engineers?"

During the question (or, more accurately, the statement and litany of questions), which lasted more than a minute, several of the drivers chuckled as it dragged on. When Koster finally stopped, Vettel opted to answer, beginning with, "Can you repeat the question?" which elicited a big laugh. He then addressed, in a good-natured manner, what Koster had asked, noting first that, "I think it [all] depends on how the monkey grows up these days."

Some interviewers engage in long, unclear preambles because they don't know what to ask next. As previously noted, it can take a while to master the ability to have a new question ready, as the interviewee heads towards the end of an answer.

In fact, many interviewees, recognizing that the interviewer is struggling, will step in and help. They might bridge the incoherent question to what they think is a logical aspect to explore, but you can't count on a helping hand.

I once had a grad student who found herself babbling during her first interview. It was with a police officer and he had no intention of saving her. All his training was to remain silent when someone was struggling with what they wanted to say, and he let her twist in the wind, as the saying goes.

Experienced interviewers can be guilty of long, unclear questions too, especially if they're nervous or intimidated. Legendary CBS journalist Dan Rather talked about this in his book, *The Camera Never Blinks*.

"President [Richard] Nixon made a habit, in a tight spot, of diverting the reporter to repeat himself," he wrote. "By doing so, he accomplished two things. He had more time to think and he put more heat on his questioner.

"I saw President Johnson do that once and I marked the tactic then as one to guard against. A reporter posed a complicated question. LBJ gave him 'The Stare,' then said flatly, 'Well, first of all, I don't think you can even repeat that question.' And the guy couldn't. He just froze. The room erupted with laughter."

During a print interview, hogging the limelight with long preambles can annoy or frustrate an interviewee; but the reader rarely, if ever, is aware that this occurred. Not so for broadcast. If they aren't edited out, they can exasperate not just the interviewee, but the audience.

KEY TAKEAWAY

- Don't use the lead-in to a question to show off how much you know about the interview topic.

FORTY-FOUR: **AVOID "UTMOST" QUESTIONS**

How would you answer these questions on the spot or during an interview, especially a broadcast?

- What's the funniest thing that's ever happened to you?
- What's the worst thing that's ever happened to you?
- What was the greatest moment in your life?
- What was the one thing that changed your life forever?

When asked these types of clichéd questions, many people pause and start to think. Wanting to be cooperative, they search their memory for the best possible response, unless one comes to mind immediately, which occasionally occurs.

The answer usually begins with the repetition of the question, to buy time. "What was the funniest thing? Gee, let me think. There were so many…"

Some people take a long time searching for the answer, which can result in a painful period of silence in a broadcast interview. I've had interviewees beg off the question and promise to get back to it later, which almost never happens.

Here's a slightly different approach: frame the question in a way that makes it easier for the person. For example:

- "Can you think of any funny experiences or stories (about the subject under discussion)?"
- "Do you recall any traumatic experiences?"
- "Were there any key events or experiences that changed your life significantly?"

By switching from an absolute to more general wording, you've made it easier for the person to access a memory.

KEY TAKEAWAY

- Resist asking the "est" questions (greatest, funniest, strangest, etc.).

FORTY-FIVE: **BAD VERBAL HABITS**

In the late 2000s, I attended a public event in downtown Toronto, at a conference on creativity.

An award-winning American artist, with more than two decades of impressive success in several different entertainment fields, was to be interviewed onstage by a woman who hosted two Canadian arts radio programs.

The artist was a delight, full of energy and enthusiasm. She had worked with major international figures in film, music, and journalism and seemed to relish her status as a role model, especially for young women.

The interviewer, however, ruined the conversation for me. Virtually every question she asked began with a concise preamble, which was good, but was followed by, "Talk to us about…"

That was not a problem the first few times, but after a while, the "talk to us about" lead-in became annoying and distracting. I began to anticipate it, which interfered with my enjoyment of the conversation.

I don't know the host and can only assume she was nervous about conducting the interview live, in front of a large number of people. Whatever the reason, she inadvertently drew attention away from the guest. Any repetitive habit will have the same result.

Broadcast-style interviews are particularly vulnerable to bad verbal habits, although the same may be said for some print interviewers. It's easy, and lazy, to rely on pat questions to get through an interview. Using them repeatedly is just not acceptable.

Starting an interview with "Tell me about yourself," or any similar vague, general wording, is usually wrong. It might elicit a good answer, but it could also render a scornful response: "What do you mean?" or "In what way?" or "Could you be a little more specific?"

I'm likewise no fan of what is often posed as a final question: "If you could do it over again, what would you do differently?"

There's nothing inherently wrong with asking that and, again, the answer could be insightful, depending on the guest. But it could also backfire. The person may decide that telling the truth would take too long or that the question is too clichéd. I don't like it because I wouldn't want to end a meaningful conversation with a trite wrap-up.

HOW DO YOU FEEL ABOUT THIS QUESTION?

One question that tends to elicit strong negative reactions in many quarters is the classic, "How do you feel?" I recall being warned, early in my career, that it was simply not asked because it was so banal.

One of Canada's most celebrated writers, Pierre Berton, especially hated it: "'How does it feel, Mrs. So-and-So? Your husband has just been murdered and your children shot. How do you feel?' Well, Christ, you know how she feels. She feels bloody awful. You shouldn't be asking questions like that. There are better ways of saying it. You say, 'Mrs. So-and-So, I know you've gone through a hard time and must feel like hell.' You establish your understanding, and you can do it with variations of that technique."

Journalist and educator Peter Desbarats, however, wondered if the question was really so bad:

"I certainly wouldn't take the position that you should never ask it. I think that for television, particularly, what you've got to convey quite often is the emotion rather than the facts. Somebody has been through a tragedy; you're trying to really show how they feel. And it may be necessary to ask people how they're feeling. I'd be very uncomfortable saying that a journalist should never say, 'How do you feel?'"

I've read posts online by people who said they yell at their TV when they hear a reporter ask the "How do you feel?" question. An aversion to the question came up in an April 2004 article in *The New York Times* about how families in the U.S. dealt with the loss of a loved one in Iraq.

One man, whose soldier brother had died under brutal circumstances, "would not discuss the details of his brother's death or how the attack—in which at least two of the four bodies were dragged through the streets and hung from a bridge in the city of Falluja, west of Baghdad—made him feel," the paper reported. "That is a question I don't want to answer," he said. "How many different types of dead are there?"

I can't imagine asking the man how he felt, if that indeed was the reporter's wording. I might have asked whether there was anything he wanted to say about what had happened.

The article said he didn't want to divulge whether his brother was married or had children: "He said it was a personal matter his family was not willing to disclose." This made it clear, to me (in considerable hindsight) that his pain was too raw to venture near the "feel" question.

I'm torn on this "feel" issue. I understand why many people agree with this post on a 2004 question-and-answer site: "One of my long-running fantasies has been to see some tiny little old lady jump up and use her handbag to beat the living bejeebus [sic] out of some reporter who had assaulted her with [the how do you feel] question. All while screaming how does that make you feel, you fucking parasite?!"

But I believe there are times when the question is warranted. The decision to use it, however, should be a clear and conscious one. Ask yourself, does this seem like the best wording for what I'm trying to accomplish? It should never be thrown out in a moment of laziness or nervousness to help the interviewer, rather than the person being questioned.

A BETTER FEEL FOR THE QUESTION

American journalist and journalism professor Dean Nelson said preparation can help an interviewer ask a better quality "How does it feel?" question:

"I think a great one that I saw not too long ago was at the end of the Stanley Cup [hockey championship]. The interviewer asked one of the players about having his dad in the rink on the day that the Stanley Cup was won. He had some sort of dementia.

"His dad didn't really know where he was, but his sheer presence in the stands was so important to the player that instead of, 'How does it feel to win the Stanley Cup?' it was, 'How does it feel to win the Stanley Cup in front of your father, who has come to all these games [and] who took you to early hockey practice when you were a kid?' Now, that really elicited humanity out of that player."

KEY TAKEAWAY

- Avoid the "How do you feel" question unless you determine that it's the best wording for the circumstances.

FORTY-SIX: **SOME PEOPLE SAY**

In October 2011, Kathleen Kelley Reardon, a professor emerita at the University of Southern California, published an article in *The Huffington Post* criticizing journalists who use phrases such as "some people say" or "many people think."

"How do we know the motives of 'some' people?" she wrote. "Who are they? Where do they come from? How many of them are there? Under what circumstances were their opinions obtained? How old are they? Did anyone pay them? Do they even exist?"

She compared the use of these vague phrases to "placing subliminal product messages in grocery store music. It's deceitful. It takes advantage of consumers." In a way, she claims, it's hearsay as journalism. FYI, I would add "it has been alleged," "a lot of people are wondering" and "some opponents claim" to the list (there are many more).

I'll suggest three reasons why journalists use this wording.

The first has to do with the history of the profession. For most of its relatively young tenure (compared to, say, medicine or law), newspapers dominated the industry. Reporters were forbidden to use the first-person singular to refer to themselves. To this day, I see newspaper accounts in which the reporter will write "A reporter observed…" or "It was noted by someone at the scene…" instead of "I saw…"

"The modern tradition of using first-person accounts in magazine features took root during the 1960s and 1970s, when journalists such as Tom Wolfe, Joan Didion, and Hunter S. Thompson, leaders of a style of reporting that came to be known as the New Journalism, began emphasizing more-literary techniques," freelance writer Knvul Sheikh wrote in *The Open Notebook*.

The practice slowly took hold in newspaper and broadcast reporting, but to a limited degree. Many reporters are still loathe to use first person.

The second, more common, reason is that it's easier and safer than naming a specific source; at least that's what the user believes. "Some people say" allows the interviewer to make an allegation or criticism without having to personalize it or find a credible source to quote.

"Some people say your decision to implement this new policy will be a disaster" is much more palatable to say to a politician than, "I think your…"

The third reason is that it often works. Many interviewees take the bait and respond to a vague allegation without challenging its source. When I worked as a media trainer, I would throw out wild allegations in mock interviews using this type of wording and the overwhelming number of participants in my sessions assumed what I was saying was true.

The problem, however, is when a savvy interviewee decides to throw it back in the interviewer's face.

Q: Some people say you're opposed to this legislation.
A: Really? Who exactly?

That's the type of response Michael Krauss, a Toronto communications consultant and president of the Hartwell Group, gives his clients: "I suggest the client calibrate his or her response, while directly asking the reporter if, in fact, the interviewer is asking the question or if 'some people' are actually saying that," he says. "I advise the client to use language such as, 'I'm pretty well plugged into that and I actually haven't heard any of the stakeholders say anything like that.'"

Barry McLoughlin, a veteran Ottawa-based media advisor, and president of TLC Transformational Leadership Consultants, concurs. When the "some people say" question comes up, he advises clients to say, "I can deal with a specific, but it's hard to deal with such a general statement."

If the interviewer can't provide a source for this type of wording, the power balance in the interview immediately shifts in the interviewee's favor.

Should you use this common tactic? It's up to you. I certainly have employed it but far less so in recent years. I prefer to have an actual source, but I have to admit the temptation to use "some people say" does exist.

KEY TAKEAWAY

- Some people say never use the "some people say" question. I mostly agree.

FORTY-SEVEN: **READING BODY LANGUAGE**

The following anecdote describes the only time in my career that an interviewee pulled out a knife during a conversation.

In the late 1980s, *Canadian Business* magazine assigned me a story about a powerful Quebec advertising agency that planned to open an office in Ontario. Traditionally, Quebec-based firms in this industry had difficulty succeeding in English Canada. Only one had prospered to date and, as part of my research, I requested an interview with the head of that firm.

The company's CEO greeted me warmly when I arrived at his Toronto office. He assured me he couldn't be happier that a major competitor would be entering the Ontario marketplace. I didn't believe him, as it didn't mesh with what I'd heard through the grapevine, but he spoke so convincingly I began to doubt my sources.

My indecision quickly ended when, at one point during our discussion, he reached into a pant pocket and took out a penknife. I watched him flip open a blade and use it to clean his fingernails with the tip. As he finished excavating a nail, he flicked the debris in my direction, all the while expressing no concerns about having a new kid enter his territory.

I'm certain he was unaware of the contradictory, and threatening, message he was sending me. I doubt he was acting consciously. I didn't mention what he was doing as we spoke because he wasn't a major character in my story. I saw no benefit in confronting him, nor did I describe the scene in my article. I thought it was so outrageous that it might distract from the rest of the article.

What his actions did do, though, was convince me that his firm was indeed apprehensive about the competition, and I found a way to incorporate that into the piece. I applied the wisdom of the 19th-century American philosopher Ralph Waldo Emerson: "When the eyes [or actions] say one thing, and the tongue another, a practiced man relies on the language of the first."

We tend to trust our instincts over our ears. That's natural, and it might even save you from harm to avoid someone whose "vibe" makes you feel uncomfortable.

If you've studied nonverbal communication to any degree you've come across the work of Albert Mehrabian, a University of California, Los Angeles psychology professor. In the 1970s, Mehrabian released findings that, he claimed, demonstrated how, in personal communications, we rely overwhelmingly on factors other than words when assessing what people are communicating to us.

He came up with a formula that is still widely referenced: 7% (words), 38% (tone of voice), 55% (body language). In other words, 93% of what we communicate doesn't come from what we say.

I have no idea whether Mehrabian was correct because I can think of numerous examples where the words were, by far, the most telling part of an interview. What I don't dispute is the importance of nonverbal information, whatever the percentages. If a used car salesman refuses to look at a vehicle he claims is an excellent purchase, I might not buy the car, no matter if it's going for a tempting price.

During interviews, I closely observe body language for any signs that help me "read" the other person. I look for significant shifts in body language, a sudden change that might illuminate how a person is reacting to a question.

For example, I recall interviewing a federal government employee about a subject I've long forgotten. What I do remember is this: I was young at the time, in my late 20s, but looked younger, and had no air of gravitas. When the interview began, the middle-aged bureaucrat was at his desk, leaning back in his chair, his arms behind his head.

He gave every indication that I was of no consequence to him. I deliberately started with some softball questions, then I asked a challenging question. At this point, he sat up in his chair and assumed a more assertive posture, immediately signaling I now had his full attention. This assured me my line of questioning was worth exploring in greater depth.

Another government employee I interviewed had been given the unfortunate task of answering questions about the common practice of awarding top census jobs to people with government connections.

A true company man, he said this never happened, but the more he lied, the more uncomfortable he became. At one point, he pulled his shirt collar away from his neck with his right index finger, as if it was too tight. The action spoke volumes about his discomfort. I pointed out what he was doing—which freaked him out—but, alas, it was a radio story, not for TV, where his nonverbal communication would have said so much.

WHAT IF YOU'RE WRONG?

One problem with reading another person's nonverbal cues? You could be wrong.

In a 2011 article in *Psychology Today* by Ronald Riggio, the Henry R. Kravis Professor of Leadership and Organizational Psychology at California's Claremont McKenna College, he wrote that it's "a common misperception that body language, or nonverbal communication, is a true 'language'—that certain nonverbal cues have clear, specific meanings and definitions. It's much more complicated than that."

He cautions against:

- Assuming that a smile is indeed a smile: "Research has shown that people—women in particular—cover discomfort with a smile."

- Believing we can tell lies from truth: "Research has shown that very few people can detect lies at levels above chance. We are simply not very good at reading complex nonverbal communications—and lies are typically complex interactions—due to misreading of cues and our stereotypes about what deception looks like. Consider: In one of our studies, we found that people actually engaged in more eye contact when lying than truth-telling, presumably because they knew the stereotypes about liars avoiding eye contact, and so they overcompensated."

- Thinking "uh" suggests nervousness: "Filling pauses with uhs...can actually be a way to improve the flow of communication. Our research found that the incidence of 'uhs' was associated with *more positive* ratings of speakers, presumably because the 'uhs' filled in the dead space between words or phrases and made the speech seem more fluid and uninterrupted."

Numerous other examples could be added to Riggio's list. I recall reading in a body language book that a male who sits in what's called the Lincoln Memorial position—legs apart, back ramrod straight, hands grasping the ends of the chair—is displaying rigidity and an unwillingness to change. That might be so; or maybe he has a bad back.

In a March 2011 article in *Forbes*, body language expert Carol Kinsey Goman told this story about her own misjudgment. "A few years ago, in New York City, I was giving a presentation to the CEO of a financial services company, outlining a speech I was scheduled to deliver to his leadership team the next day. And it wasn't going well.

"Our meeting lasted almost an hour, and through that entire time the CEO sat at the conference table with his arms tightly crossed. He didn't once smile or nod encouragement. When I finished, he said thank you (without making eye contact) and left the room.

"I was positive that his nonverbal communication was telling me that my speaking engagement would be canceled. But when I walked to the elevator, the CEO's assistant came to tell me how impressed her boss had been with my presentation. I was shocked and asked how he would have reacted had he *not* liked it. 'Oh,' said the assistant, her smile acknowledging that she had previously seen that reaction as well. 'He would have gotten up in the middle of your presentation and walked out!'

"The only nonverbal signals that I had received from that CEO were ones I judged to be negative. What I didn't realize was that, for this individual, this was normal behavior."

I learned how easy it is to misread nonverbal behavior while working on *Fraud Squad TV*. The program needed permission from the FBI to interview some of their agents. This required several of us, including the executive producer, to attend a meeting at the Bureau's headquarters in Washington. It's a massive and intimidating building, with no names on offices or signs to indicate where you are.

Our exec, a charming man, was used to people liking him—laughing at his jokes, for example. He also trusted his ability to read people. After his lengthy presentation to a room of about a dozen agents, we left to await their decision. "They hated us," he said as we debriefed. "I've never had less reaction in my life. There's no chance they will agree."

I wasn't so sure. I said: "Have you watched [the TV series] *Criminal Minds*? Agent Aaron Hotchner, especially, shows no emotion. That's what they're trained to do. I wouldn't assume." I was right. They had indeed liked us, and we were given permission to conduct our interviews.

WOMEN'S INTUITION

In their 2006 book, The Definitive Book of Body Language: The Hidden Meaning Behind People's Gestures and Expressions, *Australian body language experts Allan and Barbara Pease wrote:*

"*Overall, women are far more perceptive than men, and this has given rise to what is commonly referred to as 'women's intuition.' Women have an innate ability to pick up and decipher nonverbal signals, as well as having an accurate eye for small details. This is why few husbands can lie to their wives and get away with it and why, conversely, most women can pull the wool over a man's eyes without his realizing it.*

"Research by psychologists at Harvard University showed how women are far more alert to body language than men. They showed short films, with the sound turned off, of a man and woman communicating, and the participants were asked to decode what was happening by reading the couple's expressions. The research showed that women read the situation accurately 87 percent of the time, while the men scored only 42 percent accuracy. Men in 'nurturing' occupations, such as artistic types, acting, and nursing, did nearly as well as the women; gay men also scored well.

"Female intuition is particularly evident in women who have raised children. For the first few years, the mother relies almost solely on the nonverbal channel to communicate with the child and this is why women are often more perceptive negotiators than men, because they practice reading signals early."

Body language is important for interviewers to observe; we should always take in every aspect of what an interviewee says and does.

If the nonverbal message contradicts the verbal it's very possible the nonverbal is the truthful one. Just be careful not to play amateur psychologist. As they say in Yorkshire, England, "There's nowt so queer as folk." People don't always behave in the way we think they should.

OUR OWN BODY LANGUAGE

I've watched interviewers hug themselves defensively while getting annoyed with an interviewee who's doing the same. It's important to focus on our own body language, too.

In fact, I recommend starting with oneself, then watching the interviewee to see what they reveal.

Imagine you're trying to persuade a union leader to reveal what might happen in an ongoing labor dispute. If your arms and legs are crossed in a defensive position, is this the best posture to assume when asking another person to speak openly?

Before I start an interview, especially in person, I'm acutely aware of where and how I sit or stand. I want to have a positive and open posture, one that encourages the other person to do the same. I'm not doing it just to influence the other person's behavior; I know that if I'm in a receptive physical state, it will help me do my job better.

KEY TAKEAWAYS

- If the nonverbal message contradicts the verbal, it's probable the nonverbal is the accurate one.
- Do try to read an interviewee's body language but know that you might be wrong.
- Be aware of your own body language during an interview.

FORTY-EIGHT: **MANAGE THE INTERVIEW**

In 2017, Harry Connick Jr., host of the talk show *Harry*, asked Oprah Winfrey to name the worst guest she ever dealt with in the more than 4,500 interviews she'd conducted in her program's 25 seasons to date. She said it wasn't a famous person but a lawyer who had written a book. (She declined to identify him or the subject of his book.)

Why was he so memorable? "He mentioned his book 29 times—and that's after I started counting," she said, underlining "29 times" with a level of animated exasperation that suggested the memory was still annoying.

"Every sentence started. 'In my book, in my book, and if you buy my book,' and so finally, around the third segment, I said, 'We all know the name of the book. Audience, tell him the name of the book…so you don't have to say the name of the book anymore.' After that, we started having a conversation."

What Winfrey did that day was to manage the interview, as I like to call it. If the lawyer's persistent self-promotion irritated her, it would almost certainly have had the same effect on her viewers. She couldn't just continue asking him questions, although it sounds as if she put up with it longer than I would have. She had to deal with what was actually going on, beyond the normal question-and-answer exchange.

Too often, interviewers ignore overt or subtle aspects of the interview that can have a negative impact on what's about to transpire or what's happening during the interview. Sometimes you can survive this ostrich approach—which likely comes out of a fear of confronting the interviewee—but more often than not it's a mistake. If a concern or problem is not dealt with as it's happening, it could weaken or even derail the interview.

BEFORE THE INTERVIEW

Some years ago, I was working on a commemorative book about a midwestern U.S. company. Most of my research involved talking to current and former employees. Almost everyone was helpful and easy to deal with, but one veteran employee, upon entering the interviewing room, greeted me in a cold and hostile manner. He had an intimidating presence, which I felt from the outset. When offered a seat, he slumped down in the chair, with his arms folded firmly across his chest.

I'd never met him before, so I hadn't done anything to warrant his demeanor. I also knew when something was so obviously wrong, I couldn't just start conducting the interview.

Therefore, I did what I'd done on numerous similar occasions—I addressed my feelings head on. "Before we start," I began, being careful not to betray anxiety or annoyance in my voice, "I want to ask if you're okay about being here today because I sense you're not happy about talking to me."

"Actually, I'm not," he said. After a few questions from me, he revealed how much he hated the company, which had a new and quite unpopular CEO. He didn't want to contribute to any project the CEO had initiated, but he'd been forced to meet with me so here he was. He said I shouldn't expect him to tell me anything of value.

I asked whether he'd always been unhappy at the company, and he said it was quite the opposite. He'd loved it until the new man came in. I didn't try to make excuses for the changes that the new CEO had implemented, nor did I agree with what the disgruntled employee was saying to try to win him over. I had no idea whether his complaints were justified.

Instead, I let him vent, a process I find helpful in situations like this, then offered him a reason to cooperate with me. "It's up to you if you want to do the interview," I said, "but I was told that you know a lot of great stories about the company's history. It would be a shame not to have them in the book, which will deal with what happened during so many of the years before the new CEO took over."

He thought about it for a moment and agreed to give it a try. He remained somewhat distant as we began talking, but when the focus was on what he called the good old days, he softened somewhat. I harvested some useful anecdotes, which I'm not sure would have been the case if I'd ignored the obvious wariness he'd displayed when he first walked in.

Sometimes, an interviewee's hostility is even more overt.

"Why should I talk to you?" a fairly senior government manager once snarled at me, when I arrived in his office. "You guys are animals. Pigs. You have no ethics." Despite having been a journalist for a decade at the time, I'd never been verbally accosted like that before.

I later learned his department's media officer had forced him to grant me an interview about a report he'd worked on. His voice dripped with so much contempt that it took me a few moments to compose myself. When I did, I asked what in retrospect was an obvious question: "Have you had a bad experience with the media?" I said it in a reasonable and, I hoped, genuinely curious tone.

Indeed he had, he replied, and began to describe what, to him, was an egregious invasion of his privacy by a TV crew that had recently interviewed him on some other matter.

It's important to mention that about a month before his bad experience, a TV cameraman, using a zoom lens, had filmed images of a confidential draft of the federal budget, as it lay open on the finance minister's desk. It was an ethical *cause célèbre.*

"They tried to do the same with me not long after that," the angry bureaucrat said. Before his interview, he said, the cameraman started taking shots of the bureaucrat's office. He especially wanted the man to sit at his desk. "He then stood behind me and was obviously trying to see whatever documents were in view. Fortunately, I had put everything important away before the crew arrived."

In the next few minutes, I explained about TV cut-aways. No dissolve edits were done in those days, and the crew needed shots of the bureaucrat from behind for editing purposes. The man, who was a quick study, almost immediately understood what I was saying. Once he knew there had been no attempt at treachery, he conceded there was nothing controversial about the interview; he calmed down and cooperated with me.

Unpleasant encounters used to be an exception. Sometimes they're couched in supposed humor, with the interviewee making a laughing reference to the media's foibles; but underneath the humor is a level of hostility and, probably, fear.

Open hostility toward the media has become a more common occurrence in recent years. Interviewers need to be aware that it could be directed at them.

WHAT IF YOU'RE ATTACKED PRIOR TO AN INTERVIEW?

Don't take an attack by an interviewee personally, unless you've done something to upset the person. In that case you'll need to address what happened. Nor should you try to stop the person from ranting. Listen carefully for clues to the source of their antagonism, although there's no guarantee something specific will emerge.

When I think the person has run out of steam (or venom), I'll say something along these lines: "You've obviously had bad experiences with the media or don't trust the profession, but I want to let you know that I'm not here to defend my profession. I know that every profession has some people who aren't ethical, but the people I work with care deeply about being fair and accurate."

At this point, I'll reference the person's profession, if applicable. If they're a politician or lawyer, for example, I'll gently mention any negative stereotypes people have of them. For a lawyer, I might say: "People make jokes all the time that suggest that all lawyers care about is money. I know that isn't true. I know many ethical and trustworthy lawyers who don't deserve to be categorized that way because of some bad apples."

I'll then bridge from the general to the personal. "I want to assure you that my goal is to get the story right, which is why I'm here talking to you. I want to suggest that we try the interview, and if at any time you don't think I'm treating you properly, just let me know and we'll stop and discuss it. All I'm asking is that you judge me on what I do and say and not on whatever other experiences or perceptions you might have."

This usually works. It does not mean backing off what might be perceived as challenging questions. It's possible the introductory rant was aimed at intimidating you, so keep that in mind.

Although your stomach might be in a knot during an attack, try to remain, or at least appear to remain, calm. It's not a common part of the job but it does happen. The bottom line, of course, is that you're not there to be verbally abused or physically intimidated so, if at any time the situation feels unsafe, err on the side of caution, and quietly announce that you need to leave. Do it in a professional manner. Then report the incident, in detail, to whatever outlet you're working for.

DURING THE INTERVIEW

As Oprah had to do with the book-pushing lawyer, you might have to interrupt an interview as it's taking place to manage a problem that has surfaced. This is obviously easier to do during a print or taped broadcast discussion, but it might also have to happen during a live interview. One example involved the U.S. late night talk show host Tom Snyder.

Snyder's guest was the film mogul Joseph E. Levine, who had produced or financed almost 500 movies during his career, including *The Graduate* and *The Producers*. "I asked how he got from being a man who ran a restaurant in Boston to one of the most successful independent movie producers," Snyder recalled. "What were the things that happened along the way? Well, Levine looked at me and said, 'I was in a movie studio in Astoria in 1939 and somebody showed me a script, and the rest is history.' And he stopped. And I looked at him and he looked at me and I looked at my watch and said, 'You know, Joe, we have 42 minutes to go here, and if you could give me a little bit of this history as we go along, it would be very, very helpful.'"

It's a judgment call as to whether you confront a guest with your sense that something is wrong beyond the typical tensions that can arise during an interview. For a print or taped broadcast interview, I usually do the following:

- Turn off the recorder/camera.
- Explain that I've stopped because I want to check in with the person.
- Say that I sense something is wrong and wonder aloud whether I've said anything to upset them (I always blame myself to soften the aggressiveness of what I'm doing; and, perhaps, I have).
- Ask if there's anything we need to discuss before continuing.

I only do this after having explored every other way to make the interview work. It's a high-risk approach, but better than ignoring what's going on and walking away upset that the interview wasn't successful. For live broadcast interviews, I pray that I can find a way as direct and as artful as Tom Snyder's approach with the taciturn Joseph Levine.

KEY TAKEAWAYS

- It's your responsibility to manage an interview.
- There's no point continuing an interview when the guest is obviously hostile, unless that's what you wanted to achieve.
- If possible, pause the interview to check in with a guest who seems upset about something you're unaware of.

FORTY-NINE: **THE MOST IMPORTANT QUESTION**

I'm convinced, after more than four decades of interviewing, that the most important thing we can say during an interview is this: "I'm sorry, I don't understand. Can you explain further what you mean?"

I know an interviewer is functioning at an advanced level when I hear this being said.

It's absolutely normal for an interviewer, who is usually not an expert in the subject under discussion, to become confused or to have trouble following an interviewee's answer, especially if the information is technical or difficult to understand.

Unfortunately, too many interviewers—afraid to reveal their inability to grasp what's being said—nod and pretend to understand when they should be admitting the opposite.

Here's what I typically say in these situations: "I'm probably a bit thick but I actually don't know what that means." Most times, the interviewee responds this way: "You're not being thick. It's actually rather complicated. Let me try explaining it this way…"

Interviewees want us to get it right, especially if they're discussing something important to them.

I don't say I understand until I do. Otherwise, how can I write about it or offer viewers a clip of an answer that, to me, is not clear?

So, don't pretend just to protect your ego; tell the truth and make sure you actually understand what the other person is trying to communicate. If you don't know what's being said, what are the chances your viewers or readers will?

KEY TAKEAWAY

- One of the most important things we can say during an interview is: "I'm sorry, I don't understand."

FIFTY: **THE FINAL QUESTION**

The following final question applies to print and broadcast interviews that are taped; it's rarely asked in a live broadcast interview.

The question is short and simple: "Is there anything I haven't asked you that you'd like to add?" or other words to that effect.

Not only does this provide a clean and logical way to end an interview, it also puts an important card on the table, one that addresses our limitations. Interviewees almost always know more about the matter under discussion than we do. By asking this question, we're offering them an opportunity to add information or opinions we neglected to ask about.

I offered that opportunity at the end of an interview with a senior CBC TV producer, for an article in *TV Guide* that he thought was likely going to be critical of a new program he'd created.

During our discussion, he sat with his arms folded and his legs crossed in an incredibly defensive manner, and exuded hostility towards me for probing key, critical points that had been made by others about his show.

When I offered him the chance at the end to say whatever he wanted, his body language abruptly changed. He unfolded his arms and legs and thanked me for providing him with a platform to add what he believed were critical points. And they were.

Over the years, I've asked a lot of people what it was like to be interviewed. Many said they wished, after the fact, they'd been asked certain questions.

"Why didn't you raise them during the interview?" I wondered.

"I didn't think I was allowed to," was the most common response. The interview structure, of one person asking the questions and the other answering, is accepted, by many, as the way the process has to be carried out. Not all interviewees abide by this, of course, especially those who've been media trained. But many do. Which makes this final question so important.

In my experience, most interviewees decline the opportunity to add anything after I've wrapped up. But some do, and what they say can be helpful.

I believe all appreciate the gesture.

KEY TAKEAWAY

- At the end of an interview (unless it's a live broadcast one, although it sometimes works in that context), ask the guest if there's anything they'd like to add that they hadn't been asked about.

ACKNOWLEDGEMENTS

I am indebted to Jeremy Lucyk, my talented and compassionate editor at Centennial College Press; Talin Vartanian, for her incisive and generous edit of my rough draft; and to Eric Murphy, Ana Ivanova, and Lindy Oughtred (who made publication of the book possible), for reading and commenting on the manuscript.

I also want to thank all the professionals (too many to name) who allowed me to interview them for this book and my previous one. Without their generous contributions, I would not have been able to write either one. Also, my appreciation to the literally thousand-plus people who have allowed me to interview them over my long career.

REFERENCES

ONE: THE PREAMBLE

"2021 Global Podcast Statistics, Demographics & Habits." *PodcastHosting.org*, 10 Apr. 2021, https://podcasthosting.org/podcast-statistics/.

Byers, Kyle. "How Many Blogs Are There? (And 141 Other Blogging Stats)." *GrowthBadger*, 2 Jan. 2022, https://growthbadger.com/blog-stats/.

Pressfield, Steven. *The War of Art: Break Through the Blocks and Win Your Inner Creative Battles*. Black Irish Entertainment, 2012.

TWO: EDUCATE YOURSELF

To read more about Larry King and his interviewing style, including more context on his infamous lack of research prior to interviews, visit:
"Larry King Still the Kid with All the Questions | CBC News." *CBC News,* CBC/Radio Canada, 21 May 2009, https://www.cbc.ca/news/entertainment/larry-king-still-the-kid-with-all-the-questions-1.857063.

"New Year's Eve 1999 - 12/31/1999 - CNN Broadcast - Part 8 - Larry King interviews the Dalai Lama." *YouTube*, uploaded by Random Stuff I Find on VHS, 18 Dec. 2020, https://www.youtube.com/watch?v=X004IBkITiU.

"Kathie Lee Gifford's epic 'Today' gaffe." *CNN*, 31 May 2012. https://www.cnn.com/videos/us/2012/05/31/today-show-martin-short-kathie-lee-gifford.hln.

THREE: BE GENUINE

Markle, Meghan. "The Losses We Share." *The New York Times*, 25 Nov. 2020, https://www.nytimes.com/2020/11/25/opinion/meghan-markle-miscarriage.html.

"Meghan reveals intense media spotlight has left her struggling to cope as a mum." *ITV News*, 18 Oct. 2019, https://www.itv.com/news/2019-10-18/meghan-prince-harry-tom-bradby-itv-african-journey-documentary.

Garvey, Marianne. "Olivia Wilde addresses controversy around her 'Richard Jewell' character." *CNN*, 13 Dec. 2019, https://www.cnn.com/2019/12/13/entertainment/olivia-wilde-richard-jewell-kathy-scruggs/index.html.

Butler, Karen. "Oprah Winfrey: I don't have one face that I present to the white world." *UPI*, 7 Aug. 2013, https://www.upi.com/Entertainment_News/Movies/2013/08/07/Oprah-Winfrey-I-dont-have-one-face-that-I-present-to-the-white-world/76851375901855/.

Columbia Journalism School. "An evening with Lester Holt ~ A conversation on Journalism Ethics with Betsy West." *YouTube*, 23 Oct. 2015, https://www.youtube.com/watch?v=adu-hSkURWE&t=798s.

His Holiness the XIV Dalai Lama. *The Art of Happiness: A Handbook For Living*. 10th Anniversary Edition, Penguin, 2009.

Ted Lasso misattributes the Walt Whitman quote in:
"The Diamond Dogs." *Ted Lasso*, season 1, episode 8, Apple TV+, 18 Sep. 2020.

You can read more about the misattribution in:
Evon, Dan. "Did 'Be Curious, Not Judgmental' Originate with Walt Whitman?" *Snopes*, 5

Aug. 2021, https://www.snopes.com/fact-check/
be-curious-not-judgmental-walt-whitman/.

FOUR: UNDERSTAND THE OTHER SIDE

Stein, Harry. "HOW '60 MINUTES' MAKES NEWS." *The
New York Times*, 6 May 1979, https://www.nytimes.
com/1979/05/06/archives/how-60-minutes-makes-
news-60-minutes.html.

Lee, Harper. *To Kill a Mockingbird*. J.B. Lippincott, 1960.

Bankhead, Tallulah. *Tallulah: My Autobiography*. Harper
& Brothers, 1952.

Silva, Horacio. "Kate the Great." *T: The New York Times
Style Magazine*, 24 Nov. 2010, https://archive.nytimes.
com/tmagazine.blogs.nytimes.com/2010/11/24/
kate-on-kate/.

Dean, Howard. Interview with Elizabeth F. Ralph
and Margaret Slattery. "Why Politicians Hate the
Press." *Politico Magazine*, May/June 2015, https://
www.politico.com/magazine/story/2015/04/22/
why-politicians-hate-the-press-117142/.

Robinson, Paul. "The Chomsky Problem." *The New
York Times*, 25 Feb. 1979, https://www.nytimes.
com/1979/02/25/archives/the-chomsky-problem-
chomsky.html.

Herman, Edward S., and Noam Chomsky. *Manufacturing
Consent: The Political Economy of Mass Media*.
Pantheon Books, 1988.

CNN. "2004: The scream that doomed Howard Dean."
YouTube, 31 July 2013, https://www.youtube.com/
watch?v=l6i-gYRAwM0.

BBC News. "Prince Andrew & the Epstein Scandal: The
Newsnight Interview." *YouTube*, 17 Nov. 2019, https://
www.youtube.com/watch?v=QtBS8COhhhM.

Hickman, Arvind. "'Prince Andrew interview will reign as masterclass in PR disasters for some time' — industry reaction." *PR Week*, 20 Nov. 2019, https://www.prweek.com/article/1666041/prince-andrew-interview-will-reign-masterclass-pr-disasters-time-industry-reaction.

If you wish to read the exact comments made by David Ahenakew in 2002, The Globe and Mail *published an article that contains a series of direct quotes. Please be advised that the comments may be upsetting:*
"Ahenakew's Speech." Editorial. *The Globe and Mail*, 10 June 2006, https://www.theglobeandmail.com/opinion/ahenakews-speech/article729999/.

"Judge finds Ahenakew not guilty in 2nd hate trial." *CBC News*, 23 Feb. 2009, https://www.cbc.ca/news/canada/saskatchewan/judge-finds-ahenakew-not-guilty-in-2nd-hate-trial-1.802574.

"Anger over Justin Bieber's Anne Frank message." *BBC*, 14 Apr. 2013, https://www.bbc.com/news/world-europe-22146859.

Silva, Horacio. "Kate the Great." *T: The New York Times Style Magazine*, 24 Nov. 2010, https://archive.nytimes.com/tmagazine.blogs.nytimes.com/2010/11/24/kate-on-kate/.

Bloomberg Quicktake: Originals. "The One Question Oprah Winfrey Says Every Guest Asked." *YouTube*, 1 Mar. 2017, https://www.youtube.com/watch?v=343kpgulUXU.

Nededog, Jethro. "Oprah says every guest asks her the same question after their interviews — but she was still shocked when Beyoncé asked it." *Insider*, 23 Sep. 2017, https://www.insider.com/oprah-winfrey-question-every-guests-asks-after-interviews-beyonce-2017-9.

FIVE: ACCEPT THE ROLE

CGTN. "Trump to CNN Reporter: 'You ask a lot of stupid questions.'" *YouTube*, 10 Nov. 2018, https://www.youtube.com/watch?v=yhKMaDL8xLE.

Kreuger, Vicki. "Let Your Questions Guide the Conversation." *The Poynter Institute for Media Studies*, 12 Sep. 2016, https://www.poynter.org/educators-students/2016/in-an-interview-let-your-questions-guide-the-conversation/.

SEVEN: LOCATION, LOCATION, LOCATION

"Bob and Ray.. Wally Ballou Interviews a Cranberry Grower in Times Square." *YouTube*, uploaded by Paul Bellefeuille, 27 Nov. 2013, https://www.youtube.com/watch?v=_pBMzx0W5Vw.

EIGHT: WHAT DO I HAVE THE RIGHT TO ASK?

"From the 60 Minutes Archive: Sarko L'Americain." *CBS News*, 30 Oct. 2007, https://www.cbsnews.com/video/from-the-60-minutes-archive-sarko-lamericain-french-president-nicolas-sarkozy/.

The Associated Press. "Sarkozy abruptly ends interview with '60 Minutes.'" *CTV News*, 29 Oct. 2007, https://www.ctvnews.ca/sarkozy-abruptly-ends-interview-with-60-minutes-1.262020.

NINE: PREPARATION

Scanlan, Chip. "How Journalists Can Become Better Interviewers." *The Poynter Institute for Media Studies*, 4 Mar. 2013, https://www.poynter.org/reporting-editing/2013/how-journalists-can-become-better-interviewers/.

*Many of the actual video clips of the Rashida Jones/
Danielle Demski exchange have been removed from the
Internet. There are a few compilations on YouTube that
contain this interaction, including (beginning at 6:25):*
Nicki Swift. "Stars Who Fired Back At Their
Interviewer On Live TV." *YouTube*, 27 Apr. 2018,
https://www.youtube.com/watch?v=GeA0iXWH_i0.

Stone, Natalie. "Jerry Seinfeld Addresses Resurfaced
Larry King Interview." *People Magazine,* 23 Jan.
2021, https://people.com/tv/jerry-seinfeld-addresses-
resurfaced-larry-king-cnn-interview/.

Shea, Courtney. "Bob McCown hits sports broadcast
milestones and is still going strong." *The Globe and
Mail*, 28 Sep. 2014, https://www.theglobeandmail.com/
arts/books-and-media/bob-mccown-hits-milestone-
as-a-sports-broadcaster-and-is-still-going-strong/
article20807657/.

Seiter, Courtney. "6 Communication Tips From Some
Of The World's Best Interviewers." *Fast Company*, 8
Jan. 2014, https://www.fastcompany.com/3026222/6-
powerful-communication-tips-from-some-of-the-
worlds-best-interviewers.

TEN: WHAT ARE YOU WALKING INTO?

McLaughlin, Paul. "Interview: CAW President Ken
Lewenza." *This Magazine*, 27 Apr. 2009, https://this.
org/2009/04/27/interview-caw-president-ken-lewenza/.

ELEVEN: ROLE-PLAYING AND VISUALIZATION

Peoples, Steve, Zeke Miller, and Bill Barrow. "Biden, Trump
take differing approaches to debate preparation."
AP News, 27 Sep. 2020, https://apnews.com/article/
election-2020-virus-outbreak-joe-biden-campaigns-

michael-pence-ee021beed099a2cf8cbd1e281617
40a1.

Pickett, Mallory. "How to Conduct Difficult Interviews." *The Open Notebook*, 11 Dec. 2018, https://www.theopennotebook.com/2018/12/11/how-to-conduct-difficult-interviews/.

Markushin, Yury. "Visualization chess training." 29 Apr. 2015, https://thechessworld.com/articles/training-techniques/vizualization-chess-training/.

Breslow, David. "Visualizing Your Best Shots." *The Golf Channel*, 7 Aug. 2003, https://www.golfchannel.com/article/david-breslow/visualizing-your-best-shots.

ProSwimwear. "Michael Phelps – The Journey – Ep 5 – Visualization." *YouTube*, 20 Aug. 2018, https://www.youtube.com/watch?v=p-mZhvxeK_k.

Olivier Poorer-Leroy, Olivier. "How Michael Phelps Used Visualization to Stay Calm Under Pressure." *YourSwimBook*, https://www.yourswimlog.com/michael-phelps-visualization/.

Maltz, Maxwell. *The New Psycho-Cybernetics*. Simon & Schuster, 1960.

Bokhari, Dean. "Psycho Cybernetics by Maxwell Maltz: Book Summary." *MeaningfulHQ*, https://www.meaningfulhq.com/psycho-cybernetics-by-maxwell-maltz.html.

TWELVE: BE CONVERSATIONAL

Dick Cavett recalls the advice from Jack Paar in:
Galanes, Philip. "Dick Cavett and Alec Baldwin Start the Conversation." *The New York Times,* 1 Nov. 2013, https://www.nytimes.com/2013/11/03/fashion/Dick-Cavett-and-Alec-Baldwin-Start-the-Conversation.html.

The Dick Cavett Show. "Gore Vidal vs Norman Mailer | The Dick Cavett Show." *YouTube*, 20 Sep. 2019, https://www.youtube.com/watch?v=Nb1w_qoioOk.

Kerr, Jolie. "How to Talk to People, According to Terry Gross." *The New York Times*, 17 Nov. 2018, https://www.nytimes.com/2018/11/17/style/self-care/terry-gross-conversation-advice.html.

Boehme, Gerry. *Henry Ford: Assembly Line and Automobile Pioneer*. Cavendish Square Publishing, 2020.

THIRTEEN: IT'S OKAY TO BE SHY

Retter, Jen. "Jennifer Retter: Using Introversion As A Weapon." *Ninja Journalism*, 18 Dec. 2013, https://ninjajournalist.blogspot.com/2013/12/i-always-enjoyed-jennifer-retters.html.

FOURTEEN: ASKING A PERSON'S AGE

Houpt, Simon. "Veteran journalist Linden MacIntyre first high-profile casualty of CBC cuts." *The Globe and Mail*, 7 May 2014, https://www.theglobeandmail.com/report-on-business/linden-macintyre-first-high-profile-casualty-of-cbc-cuts/article18544290/.

FIFTEEN: WE'RE NOT THE POLICE

60 Minutes Staff. "A surprise interview, explained." *CBS News*, 2 June 2013, https://www.cbsnews.com/news/a-surprise-interview-explained/.

"May 21, 2006." *Reliable Sources*, CNN, https://transcripts.cnn.com/show/rs/date/2006-05-21/segment/01.

"Journalistic Standards and Practices." *CBC News*, https://cbc.radio-canada.ca/en/vision/governance/journalistic-standards-and-practices.

For more about Bob McKeown's 2005 interview with David Frost, and resulting documentaries:
"CBC uncovers Danton-frost intrigue." *CBC Sports*, 18 Apr. 2006, https://www.cbc.ca/sports/hockey/cbc-uncovers-danton-frost-intrigue-1.560650.

Evans, Brooke. "An Overview of the Food Lion v ABC (1999): By Brooke Evans." *Harvard Law*, Apr. 2016, https://h2o.law.harvard.edu/text_blocks/27512.

"The landmark Food Lion case." *The Reporters Commitment for Freedom of the Press*, https://www.rcfp.org/journals/news-media-and-law-spring-2012/landmark-food-lion-case/.

Marx, Greg. "The Ethics of Undercover Journalism: Why Journalists Get Squeamish over James O'Keefe's Tactics." *The Columbia Journalism Review*, 4 Feb. 2010, https://archives.cjr.org/campaign_desk/the_ethics_of_undercover_journalism.php.

The entirety of Bob Steele's checklist (https://www.poynter.org/news/deceptionhidden-cameras-checklist) *has been removed from the Internet, but it is cited in numerous other sources.*

SEVENTEEN: INVASIVE PERSONAL QUESTIONS AND SEXISM

Extratv. "'The Avengers' Interviews: Scarlet Johansson and Jeremy Renner." *YouTube*, 3 May 2012, https://www.youtube.com/watch?v=DHxzxgwJTFc.

Kearns, Megan. "Cross-Post: Quote of the Day: Scarlett Johansson Tired of Sexist Diet Questions." *Women and*

Hollywood, 1 June 2012, https://womenandhollywood. com/cross-post-quote-of-the-day-scarlett-johansson-tired-of-sexist-diet-questions-f28c7de0c3a2/.

McCall, Marjorie. "Ariana Grande Blasts DJ's for sexist question 'You need a little brushing up on quality.'" *Billboard*, 3 Nov. 2015, https://www.billboard.com/music/pop/ariana-grande-sexist-power-106-radio-interview-video-6752937/.

Blasberg, Derek. "Emma Watson, Rebel Belle." *Vanity Fair*, 28 Feb. 2017, https://www.vanityfair.com/hollywood/2017/02/emma-watson-cover-story.

"Actress Emma Watson says revealing photo does not undermine feminism." *Reuters*, 5 Mar. 2017, https://www.reuters.com/article/us-people-emmawatson-idUSKBN16C0QV.

"Michael Jackson - Talks to Oprah (February 10, 1993)." *YouTube*, uploaded by MJ Live & Rare Videos, 10 Feb. 2022, https://www.youtube.com/watch?v=KvwAz57edv0.

"The Michael Jackson Interview: Oprah Reflects." *Oprah Magazine*, 16 Sep. 2009, https://www.oprah.com/entertainment/oprah-reflects-on-her-interview-with-michael-jackson/all.

Freeman, Hadley. "Why do so many male journalists think female stars are flirting with them." *The Guardian* 2 Mar. 2017, https://www.theguardian.com/fashion/2017/mar/20/male-journalists-female-stars-flirting-vogue-profile-selena-gomez-interviewing.

Cohen, Rich. "Alicia Silverstone: Ballad of a Teenage Queen." *Rolling Stone*, 7 Sep. 1995, https://www.rollingstone.com/feature/alicia-silverstone-ballad-of-a-teenage-queen-191633/.

Cohen, Rich. "Welcome to the Summer of Margot Robbie." *Vanity Fair*, 6 July 2016, https://www.vanityfair.com/hollywood/2016/07/margot-robbie-cover-story.

Harmon, Steph. "Margot Robbie calls her *Vanity Fair* profile 'really weird.'" *The Guardian*, 26 July 2016, https://www.theguardian.com/film/2016/jul/26/margot-robbie-calls-her-vanity-fair-profile-really-weird.

Thom Senzee, Thom. "7 Lessons on How (and How Not) to Interview Transpeople." *The Advocate*, 24 Apr. 2015, https://www.advocate.com/politics/media/2015/04/24/7-lessons-how-and-how-not-interview-trans-people.

McCormick, Joseph. "Trans actress Laverne Cox: 'a Preoccupation with Transition and Surgery Objectifies Trans People.'" *PinkNews*, 9 Jan. 2014, https://www.pinknews.co.uk/2014/01/09/trans-actress-laverne-cox-a-preoccupation-with-transition-and-surgery-objectifies-trans-people/.

Just Not Sports. "#MoreThanMean - Women in Sports 'Face' Harassment." *YouTube*, 26 Apr. 2016, https://www.youtube.com/watch?v=9tU-D-m2JY8.

EIGHTEEN: INTERVIEWEE DEMANDS

Kent, Thomas. "Should Journalists Let Sources Look Over Stories Before Publication." *The Poynter Institute for Media Studies*, 12 May 2020, https://www.poynter.org/reporting-editing/2020/should-journalists-let-sources-look-over-stories-before-publication/.

NINETEEN: WHEN DIFFICULT CONDITIONS ARE IMPOSED

Stoynoff, Natasha. "Physically attacked by Donald Trump – a PEOPLE Writer's Own Harrowing Story." *People*

Magazine, 12 Oct. 2016, https://people.com/politics/
donald-trump-attacked-people-writer/.

*Stoynoff's interview with Peirce Brosnan was originally
published in* People *Magazine, but can be read in an
archive of Pierce Brosnan interviews at:*
Stoynoff, Natasha. "People Magazine." *Pierce Brosnan
Files,* 23 Jan. 2006, http://pbfiles.net/interviews/
Inter040-People.html.

Flegenheimer, Matt. "What Does 'Off the Record' Really
Mean?" *The New York Times,* 2 Aug. 2018, https://
www.nytimes.com/2018/08/02/reader-center/off-the-
record-meaning.html.

TWENTY: COMFORT THE AFFLICTED/ AFFLICT THE COMFORTABLE

Greenwald, Glenn. "Edward Snowden's worst
fear has not been realised – thankfully."
The Guardian, 14 June 2013, https://www.
theguardian.com/commentisfree/2013/jun/14/
edward-snowden-worst-fear-not-realised.

Powers, Ron. "Interview: Walter Cronkite." *Playboy,* June
1973.

Löffelholz, Martin. "embedded journalism". *Encyclopedia
Britannica,* 6 June 2016, https://www.britannica.com/
topic/embedded-journalism. Accessed 1 August 2022.

Chomsky, Noam, and David Barsamian. *Imperial
Ambitions: Conversations with Noam Chomsky on the
Post-9/11 World.* Metropolitan Books, 2006.

Brad Wheeler, Brad. "Is Neil Diamond Cool Again?"
The Globe and Mail, 18 Nov. 2005, https://www.
theglobeandmail.com/arts/is-neil-diamond-cool-again/
article22506719/.

TWENTY-TWO: TRUST AND RAPPORT

Gibbons, Serenity. "You and Your Business Have 7 Seconds to Make a First Impression: Here's How to Succeed." *Forbes Magazine*, 19 June 2018, https://www.forbes.com/sites/serenitygibbons/2018/06/19/you-have-7-seconds-to-make-a-first-impression-heres-how-to-succeed/?sh=328f54cb56c2.

Nelson, Audrey. "The Politics of Eye Contact: a Gender Perspective." *Psychology Today*, 15 Sep. 2010, https://www.psychologytoday.com/ca/blog/he-speaks-she-speaks/201009/the-politics-eye-contact-gender-perspective.

Greengross, Gil. "Want to Increase Trust in Others? Just Smile." *Psychology Today*, 30 Apr. 2015, https://www.psychologytoday.com/us/blog/humor-sapiens/201504/want-increase-trust-in-others-just-smile-0.

"Gillian Anderson at David Letterman's show 2008." *YouTube*, uploaded by GA Edits, 8 May 2020, https://www.youtube.com/watch?v=HJgUKvHDdwI.

Andrei Harmsworth, Andrei. "Anderson: Clinton Gave Me the Eye." *Metro*, 30 July 2008, https://metro.co.uk/2008/07/30/anderson-clinton-gave-me-the-eye-326546/.

TWENTY-THREE: LISTENING

Peck, M. Scott. *The Road Less Traveled: A New Psychology of Love, Traditional Values and Spiritual Growth*. Arrow Books, 1978.

Lisa Firestone, Lisa. "One Proven Way to Feel Close to Your Partner Right Now." *Psychology Today*, 24 Sep. 2019, https://www.psychologytoday.com/us/blog/compassion-matters/201909/the-one-proven-way-feel-close-your-partner-right-now.

"Peter Drucker: Father of Modern Management." *A World of Ideas*, 17 Nov. 1988, https://billmoyers.com/content/peter-drucker/. Transcript.

Stephanie Vozza, Stephanie. "6 Reasons Why You're a Bad Listener (and How to Change It)." *Fast Company,* 28 Jan. 2019, https://www.fastcompany.com/90293558/6-reasons-why-youre-a-bad-listener-and-how-to-change-it.

Covey, Stephen R. *The 7 Habits of Highly Effective People: Powerful Lessons in Personal Change.* Free Press, 1989.

Hemingway, Ernest. "Monologue to the Maestro: A High Seas Letter." *Esquire*, Oct. 1935.

TWENTY-FOUR: SILENCE

Sachs, Albert L. *The Jail Diary of Albie Sachs.* McGraw-Hill, 1967.

"Louis Theroux in Conversation." *Southbank Centre's Book Podcast,* 20 Sep. 2019, https://www.southbankcentre.co.uk/blog/podcasts/book-podcast-louis-theroux-conversation.

Turner, Graham. *The Power of Silence: The Riches That Lie Within.* Bloomsbury, 2012.

Scanlan, Chip. "How Journalists Can Become Better Interviewers." *The Poynter Institute for Media Studies*, 4 Mar. 2013, https://www.poynter.org/reporting-editing/2013/how-journalists-can-become-better-interviewers/.

TWENTY-FIVE: TONE

OWN. "How Daniel Day-Lewis Found Abraham Lincoln's Voice | Oprah's Next Chapter | Oprah Winfrey Network." *YouTube*, 3 Dec. 2012, https://www.youtube.com/watch?v=5g9v8y5FvSo.

Lickerman, Alex. "The Importance of Tone." *Psychology Today*, 5 Aug. 2010, https://www.psychologytoday.com/ca/blog/happiness-in-world/201008/the-importance-tone.

Jaekl, Philip. "The real reason the sound of your own voice makes you cringe." *The Guardian*, 12 July 2018, https://www.theguardian.com/science/2018/jul/12/the-real-reason-the-sound-of-your-own-voice-makes-you-cringe.

Mehrabian, Albert. *Silent Messages: Implicit Communication of Emotions and Attitudes*. Wadsworth Publishing Company, 1972.

Zlevor, Greg. "The Power of Tone." *The Association for Power Development*, 23 Oct. 2018, https://www.td.org/insights/the-power-of-tone.

"Savvy detective praised for Williams confession." *CBC News*, 21 Oct. 2010, https://www.cbc.ca/news/canada/savvy-detective-praised-for-williams-confession-1.869240.

CBC News. "Russell Williams - The Confession - the fifth estate." *YouTube*, 5 Sep. 2014, https://www.youtube.com/watch?v=lj7QRP37Wn0.

TWENTY-SEVEN: OPEN AND CLOSED QUESTIONS

Mullins, Lisa. "Want to Know How to Ask Questions? Longtime Journalist Shows How It's Done in New Book." *WBUR*, 8 Mar. 2019, https://www.wbur.org/hereandnow/2019/03/08/dean-nelson-interviewing.

Scanlan, Chip. "How Journalists Can Become Better Interviewers." *The Poynter Institute for Media Studies*, 4 March 2013, https://www.poynter.org/reporting-editing/2013/how-journalists-can-become-better-interviewers/.

Katsnelson, Alla. "Interviewing for Career-Spanning Profiles." *The Open Notebook*, 27 Mar. 2018, https://www.theopennotebook.com/2018/03/27/interviewing-for-career-spanning-profiles/.

THIRTY-ONE: SLOW DOWN

Jacobs, Fred. "The Power of Dead Air." *Jacobs Media*, 28 Mar. 2018, https://jacobsmedia.com/power-dead-air/.

Bashore Jr., Theodore R. et al. "Response-specific slowing in older age revealed through differential stimulus and response effects on P300 latency and reaction time." *Neuropsychology, development, and cognition,* vol. 21, no. 6, 2014, pp. 633-73. DOI: 10.1080/13825585.2013.850058.

Ciaramicoli, Arthur. *The Stress Solution: Using Empathy and Cognitive Behavioral Therapy to Reduce Anxiety and Develop Resilience*. New World Media, 2016.

Norman, Matt. "What is Slow Journalism." *National Geographic*, 20 Feb. 2017, https://www.nationalgeographic.org/projects/out-of-eden-walk/blogs/lab-talk/2017-02-what-slow-journalism/.

THIRTY-TWO: DON'T ANSWER YOUR OWN QUESTIONS

"Aug 19: Remembering Dave Hawerchuk." Podcast from Sportsnet, 19 Aug. 2020, https://podcast.sportsnet.ca/uncategorized/aug-19-remembering-dave-hawerchuk/.

"Journalist Tricks and Traps: 10 Types of Questions to Prepare for Before an Interview." *Media First*, 10 Sep. 2013, https://www.mediafirst.co.uk/blog/journalist-tricks-and-traps-10-types-of-questions-to-prepare-for-before-an-interview/.

THIRTY-THREE: INTERVIEWEE FATIGUE

Hiscock, John. "Harrison Ford on Fame, Family, and Fortune: Retirement is For Old People." *DailyMirror*, 10 Sep. 2013, https://www.mirror.co.uk/3am/celebrity-news/harrison-ford-fame-family-fortune-2263184.

Susman, Gary. "Tales of the junket." *The Guardian*, 5 Oct. 2001, https://www.theguardian.com/film/2001/oct/05/pressandpublishing.artsfeatures.

TEDx Talks. "The Art Of Asking Questions | Dan Moulthrop | TEDxSHHS." *YouTube*, 18 Dec. 2015, https://www.youtube.com/watch?v=hZSY0PssqH0.

THIRTY-FOUR: THE BROADCAST INTERVIEW

"Hugh Grant interview Tonight Show 1995." *YouTube*, uploaded by Hermant Patel, 5 Oct. 2013, https://www.youtube.com/watch?v=vrJ2jc6qfzA.

Riemenschneider, Chris. "Actor Hugh Grant 'Fesses up to Leno on *Tonight Show*.'" *Los Angeles Times*, 11 July 1995, https://www.latimes.com./archives/la-xpm-1995-07-11-me-22547-story.html.

"ABC's 20/20 full interview with Monica Lewinsky (3 March 1999)." *YouTube*, uploaded by be prof, 31 Mar. 2019, https://www.youtube.com/watch?v=vUUATD_pfYE.

Jensen, Elizabeth. "Not the Usual 20/20 Interview." *Los Angeles Times*, 3 Mar. 1999, https://www.latimes.com/archives/la-xpm-1999-mar-03-ca-13381-story.html.

"Whitney Houston Tells Diane Sawyer: 'Crack Is Whack.'" *ABC News*, 13 Nov. 2002, https://abcnews.go.com/Entertainment/whitney-houston-tells-diane-sawyer-crack-whack/story?id=131898.

"Transcript: Whitney Houston: 'I'm a Person Who Has Life.'" *ABC News*, 13 Feb. 2012, https://abcnews.go.com/Entertainment/transcript-whitney-houston-im-person-life/story?id=15574357. Transcript.

Eames, Tom. "Sir David Frost: 'TV interviews are a power struggle.'" *Digital Spy*, 13 Mar. 2012, https://www.digitalspy.com/tv/a370829/sir-david-frost-tv-interviews-are-a-power-struggle/.

THIRTY-SIX: TELEPHONE AND EMAIL INTERVIEWS

Freeman, Hadley. "I've enjoyed talking to celebrities from my bed. Will I want to do it in person again?" *The Guardian*, 26 Dec. 2020, https://www.theguardian.com/commentisfree/2020/dec/26/ive-enjoyed-talking-to-celebrities-from-my-bed-will-i-want-to-do-it-in-person-again.

THIRTY-EIGHT: DIFFICULT INTERVIEWS

Q on cbc. "Billy Bob Thornton 'Blow Up' on Q TV." *YouTube*, 8 Apr. 2009, https://www.youtube.com/watch?v=IJWS6qyy7bw.

A breakdown of this exchange is available at: "Billy Bob blow-by-blow." *The Toronto Star*, 9 April 2009, https://www.thestar.com/entertainment/2009/04/09/billy_bob_blowbyblow.html.

Gian Ghomeshi's criminal case remains one of the most controversial episodes in Canadian media history. There are innumerable sources discussing the allegations, trial, acquittal, and impact on both the legal and media landscape. Please be aware that some of the information could be triggering.

For a detailed examination of the subject:
Kingston, Anne. "What Jian Ghomeshi did." *Maclean's*, 30 Mar. 2016, https://www.macleans.ca/news/canada/what-jian-ghomeshi-did/.

A Portrait of the Press, Warts and All. Directed by Thomas Tomizawa, produced by John Chancellor, NBC News, 1985.

George Lincoln Rockwell's appearance on This Hour Has Seven Days *is not readily accessible, but you can read about the furor it provoked at the time:*
"CANADIANS ASSAIL GOVERNMENT'S TV; Its Interview With Rockwell Stirs Commons Debate." *The New York Times*, 1 Nov. 1964, https://www.nytimes.com/1964/11/01/archives/canadians-assail-governments-tv-its-interview-with-rockwell-stirs.html.

Eskenazi, Gerald. "The Art of the Tough Interview." *Columbia Journalism Review*, 28 Sep. 2015, https://www.cjr.org/first_person/the_art_of_the_tough_interview.php.

"Transcript: Whitney Houston: 'I'm a Person Who Has Life.'" *ABC News*, 13 Feb. 2012, https://abcnews.go.com/Entertainment/transcript-whitney-houston-im-person-life/story?id=15574357. Transcript.

A transcript of Linda MacLennan's interview with Margaret Thatcher is available at:
"TV Interview for CTV." *Margaret Thatcher Foundation*, https://www.margaretthatcher.org/document/106264.

FORTY: WHAT IF THEY QUESTION ME?

"Helen Mirren - The sexist Parkinson's interview [1/2]."
   YouTube, uploaded by beretsheri0001, 22 Mar. 2008,
   https://www.youtube.com/watch?v=gmlP_cFOoAM.

"Helen Mirren - The sexist Parkinson's interview [2/2]."
   YouTube, uploaded by beretsheri0001, 22 Mar. 2008,
   https://www.youtube.com/watch?v=qRVuqjbrj4k.

FORTY-ONE: INTERVIEWING VICTIMS

Gibb, Don. "The Final Word On A Life Lived." *Media
   Magazine*, vol. 15, 2012, pp. 7-8, https://j-source.ca/
   embracing-the-deadbeat-the-final-word-on-a-life-lived/.

Pimenta, Merissa. "Tips for Reporters when Working with
   Victims of Violent Crime." *Victims for Justice*, Apr. 1,
   2019, https://victimsforjustice.org/2019/04/01/tips-for-
   reporters-when-working-with-victims-of-violent-crime/.

"Reporting on Sexual Violence: A Guide for Journalists."
   Minnesota Coalition Against Sexual Assault, 2004,
   https://barcc.org/assets/pdf/Journalists-a_guide.pdf.

"If the Media Calls: A Guide for Crime Victims &
   Survivors." *Canadian Resource Centre for Victims
   of Crime*, 2004, https://crcvc.ca/wp-content/
   uploads/2021/09/if-the-media-calls.html-charsetutf-8.

"Portraits of Grief" are still available through The New
   York Times *archive, as well updates written for the ten-
   year anniversary of 9/11:*
   https://archive.nytimes.com/www.nytimes.com/
   interactive/us/sept-11-reckoning/portraits-of-grief.html.

English, Kathy. "What readers should know about
   journalism." *The Toronto Star*, 31 Dec. 2018, https://
   www.thestar.com/opinion/public_editor/2018/12/31/
   what-readers-should-know-about-journalism.html.

FORTY-TWO: INTERVIEWING MINORS

Carr, Sarah. "Interviewing Children: An EWA Guide for Reporters." *Education Writers Association,* 18 Dec. 2012, https://www.ewa.org/webinar/interviewing-children-ewa-guide-reporters. Webinar.

Neason, Alexandria. "Conducting interviews with kids: Do's and don'ts." *Columbia Journalism Review*, 15 Mar. 2018, https://www.cjr.org/analysis/kids-interview-journalism.php.

FORTY-THREE: LONG PREAMBLES

FORMULA 1. "The Longest Press Conference Question Ever?! | 2014 Abu Dhabi Grand Prix." *YouTube*, 23 Nov. 2017, https://www.youtube.com/watch?v=FlFt_W4664M.

Rather, Dan. *The Camera Never Blinks: Adventures of a TV Journalist.* William Morrow & Co., 1977.

FORTY-FIVE: BAD VERBAL HABITS

Sabrina Tavernise, Sabrina, and Jo Napolitano. "The Struggle for Iraq: grief, mostly in private, for 4 lives brutally ended." *The New York Times*, 2 Apr. 2004, https://www.nytimes.com/2004/04/02/us/struggle-for-iraq-families-grief-mostly-private-for-4-lives-brutally-ended.html.

Languagehat. Comment on "Media & Arts." Ask Metafilter, 2 April 2004, 12:56 p.m., https://ask.metafilter.com/6244/How-do-you-feel.

Mullins, Lisa. "Want to Know How to Ask Questions? Longtime Journalist Shows How It's Done in New Book." *WBUR*, 8 Mar. 2019, https://www.wbur.org/hereandnow/2019/03/08/dean-nelson-interviewing.

FORTY-SIX: SOME PEOPLE SAY

Reardon, Kathleen. "The High Political Price of 'Some People Say' Journalism." *Huffington Post*, 17 Oct. 2011, https://www.huffpost.com/entry/the-high-political-price_b_1015843.

Sheikh, Knvul. "Journalists as Characters: Using First Person Narration to Drive Stories." *The Open Notebook*, 30 Apr. 2019, https://www.theopennotebook.com/2019/04/30/journalists-as-characters-using-first-person-narration-to-drive-stories/.

FORTY-SEVEN: READING BODY LANGUAGE

"Albert Mehrabian." *British Library*, https://www.bl.uk/people/albert-mehrabian.

Riggio, Ronald E. "Four Mistakes We Make Reading Body Language." *Psychology Today*, 20 Dec. 2011, https://www.psychologytoday.com/ca/blog/cutting-edge-leadership/201112/four-mistakes-we-make-reading-body-language.

Goman, Carol Kinsey. "The Mistakes People Make Reading Your Body Language." *Forbes Magazine*, 1 Mar. 2011, https://www.forbes.com/sites/carolkinseygoman/2011/03/01/the-mistakes-people-make-reading-your-body-language/?sh=641beda09c0f.

Pease, Barbara, and Allan Pease. *The Definitive Book of Body Language: The Hidden Meaning Behind People's Gestures and Expressions*. Bantam, 2006.

FORTY-EIGHT: MANAGE THE INTERVIEW

Harry Connick Jr. "Oprah On Her Most Annoying Talk Show Guests." *YouTube*, 7 Nov. 2017, https://www.youtube.com/watch?v=mfOosZ1mBow.

INDEX

SUBJECT INDEX

adaptability, improvisation,
    44, 49, 212-213,
    246-247
age,
    interviewee,
        46, 102-104, 117, 153,
        193, 219, 220, 257-261
    interviewer, 46, 101
    seniors, 46, 103-4, 153, 193
    minors, 257-261
allegations/unproven fact,
    87, 92, 93, 131, 274-275
bias, 47
    objectivity vs. subjectivity,
    143-144
broadcast (vs. print), 65-66,
    182-183, 196-197, 207-
    215, 262-263, 294-295
conflict (potential in interviews),
    22-23, 81, 86-94, 121,
    209, 222, 237, 284-291
crime, 72-73, 252-255
    Mob/Mafia, 91-92
culture, and cultural barriers,
    46, 102, 165

D&A (details and anecdotes),
    181, 184-190, 219, 228
discrimination, 190
    homophobia, 69, 159, 248
    racism, 116, 236-237
    sexism, 115-123
distraction, 158, 161, 225
drugs, 69, 133, 135, 208
email, 53, 54, 55, 59, 224,
    228, 229, 254
emotion, emotional content,
    60-61, 68, 91-94, 147,
    166, 168, 170, 181, 199,
    209, 214, 219, 248, 256,
    270
ethics, 25, 34, 63, 92, 105,
    137, 222, 288, 289
fake news, 22-23
gender, 25, 46, 118-119, 122,
    123
hijacking (of interview),
    48, 284-291
Holocaust, the,
    43, 144, 168-169

interruptions, interrupting,
48-50, 74, 75, 187, 193,
213, 289
jargon, 43, 44, 135, 261
knowledge,
general, 29-31
specific (interview prep),
23, 28-29, 32, 41, 46-
47, 71-79, 81, 91, 101,
189, 216
language, 25, 43-46, 165, 193,
198, 261
body language, 75, 147,
148, 151, 193, 203,
217, 225, 230, 276-
283, 294
law enforcement, 26, 61, 145,
146, 149, 264
FBI, 34, 188, 281
listening, 23, 24, 75, 78, 100,
121, 148, 156-163, 181,
192, 195, 212, 214, 215,
217, 225, 227, 288
verbal listening, 215
location(s),
60-66, 219, 221, 224,
257, 261
media,
communications and PR
departments, specialists,
51, 52, 58-59, 68, 124,
125-126, 142, 151,
274, 277, 279

training, message track,
48, 113, 137, 145, 166,
180, 211, 213, 222,
226, 264, 295
media depictions of
interviews, 34-35, 100
New Journalism, 274
nonverbal communication,
151, 155, 174, 276-280
off the record, 135-138, 179,
222
personal safety, comfort,
25, 38, 65, 68, 106, 134,
152, 165-166, 187, 218,
225, 240, 259, 277-278,
289
posture, 147-148, 211, 219,
225, 261, 278, 280, 283
preconditions (for interviews),
132-134
preparation, 23, 31, 71-79,
80-81, 86, 88, 90, 91,
93, 101, 174, 203, 226,
241, 272
print (vs. broadcast),
19, 60, 64, 99, 101, 141,
142, 181, 182, 184, 187,
196, 205, 207, 209, 210,
211, 216-223, 240, 265,
269, 289, 290, 294
questions,
open and closed questions,
178-179, 196-200

feeding questions, 196-200

rapport, building (trust), 38, 132, 136, 146, 147-148, 150-155, 217, 222-223

religion, 204

research, 23, 28-29, 41, 46, 47, 71-72, 74, 78, 87, 91, 94, 97, 101, 189, 197, 209, 216, 285,

science, scientists, 43-45, 47, 73-74, 209

sex/sexuality/relationships/ sexism, 35, 41, 69, 115-123, 152, 207, 234, 252, 262

social media, 21, 53, 54, 55, 59, 79, 102, 165, 261

sound (ambient, silence), 64-66, 156, 164-169, 182, 191-193, 246, 266

sports, sports journalism, 32, 76, 78, 112, 152, 153, 160, 196, 263
    football, 112
    golf, 45, 89, 103, 262
    hockey, 108, 120, 126, 153-154, 196, 205, 253, 272
    Olympics, 34, 89, 153
    sideline mode/performance mode, 112-114

tone (of voice), 24, 45, 84, 106, 148, 156, 170-175, 197, 218, 222, 234-236, 240, 258, 260, 277, 287

trauma, 33, 93-94, 168, 180, 187, 248-256, 258-259, 261, 267, 271

truth/deception, 91, 105-111, 141, 145-149, 170, 269, 279, 282

unions (CAW), 80, 178, 283

wording, 44-45, 49, 54, 75, 88-89, 90, 91, 93, 106, 129, 148-149, 189, 196-200, 212-213, 236, 240, 244, 253, 267, 269-272, 273-275, 294

NAME INDEX

Ahenakew, David, 42, 302

Albee, Edward, 83

Alley, Kirstie, 203

Anderson, Gillian, 152

Andrew, Prince (Andrew Windsor), 41-42

Anka, Paul, 91-92

Avila, Eva, 201

Bale, Christian, 117

Bamberger, Michael, 262

Banaszyski, Jacqui, 181

Bankhead, Tallulah, 39

Barrie, Andy, 166

Benmergui, Ralph, 159, 203, 204, 211

Bennett, Tony, 202

Berton, Pierre, 64, 269

Beyoncé (Knowles), 46, 202

Biden, Joe, 86

Bieber, Justin, 43

Brosnan, Pierce, 132-133

Burke, Brian, 196

Burns, Pat, 125-126

Byrnes, Frank, 145, 236

Callwood, June, 128

Cantor, Eddie, 195

Carlos the Jackal, 109

Cavett, Dick, 96-97

Chomsky, Noam, 40-41, 143

Ciaramicoli, Arthur, 194

Clinton, Bill, 151-152, 208

Cohen, Rich, 118

Comey, James, 188

Connick Jr., Harry, 284

Couric, Katie, 122

Covey, Stephen, 161

Cox, Laverne, 122

Cribb, Roy, 88

Cronkite, Walter, 142-143

Crosbie, Andrew, 52

Cutler, Dave, 112-113

Dalai Lama, the, 28, 37, 77

Danton, Mike, 108

Davidi, Shi, 32, 136, 160, 242

Davis, Greena, 227

Day-Lewis, Daniel, 170, 175

Dean, Howard, 40, 41

Debussy, Claude, 168

Demski, Danielle, 77

Desbarats, Peter, 225

Diamond, Neil, 144

Didion, Joan, 274

Donahue, Phil, 36

Downey Jr., Robert, 115-117

Drapeau, Jean, 167

Drucker, Peter, 160

Einstein, Albert, 75

ElBaradei, Mohamed, 57

Epstein, Jeffrey, 41

Eskenazi, Gerald, 238-239

Faldo, Nick, 45

Fellini, Federico, 169

Flegenheimer, Matt, 135

Foerster, Heinz von, 143

Ford, Harrison, 202

Freeman, Hadley,
    118-119, 227

Frost, David (coach), 108

Frost, David (journalist),
    162, 210

Ghomeshi, Jian, 232-234

Gibb, Don, 248-250

Gifford, Kathie Lee, 28-29

Ginsberg, Allen, 204

Goman, Carol Kinsey, 280

Grande, Ariana, 116

Grant, Hugh, 207

Greenwald, Glenn, 140

Gretzky, Wayne, 205

Gross, Terry, 97

Gzowski, Peter, 171

Haggard, Ted, 69

Halstead, Fred, 161

Harris, Robert, 55

Harron, Don, 171

Harry, Prince
    (Henry Windsor), 33

Hathaway, Anne, 117

Hawerchuk, Dale, 196

Hayes, David, 31

Holt, Lester, 36

Houston, Whitney, 208

Hoyt, Robert, 236

Jackson, Michael, 116

Jacobs, Fred, 192

Jewell, Richard, 34

Johansson, Scarlett, 115-117

Jones, Rashida, 77

Kent, Thomas, 130

Kim, Jean, 199

King, Larry, 28, 77-78

Koster, Walter, 263-264

Krauss, Michael, 274

Leiterman, Douglas, 236-237

Leno, Jay, 207

Letterman, David, 53, 152, 207

Levine, Joseph E., 290-291

Lewenza, Ken, 80

Lewinsky, Monica, 208

Lewis, Jerry,
    74, 170, 175

Liebling, A. J., 73

Lombardi, Vince, 49

Lomez, Céline, 65

Luce, Henry, 143

Lynn, Fred, 238-239

MacGregor, Roy,
    71, 158, 217

MacIntyre, Linden, 103

MacLennan, Linda, 241-242

MacNeil, Robert, 192, 237

Mailer, Norman, 97, 306

Maitlis, Emily, 41

Malling, Eric, 168, 238

Maltz, Maxwell, 94

Markle, Meghan, 33

Maron, Marc, 78

McCabe, Andrew, 188

McCown, Bob, 78

McGowan, Mike, 125-126

McKenna, Terence, 88

McKeown, Bob,
    55-57, 108-109

McLean, Stuart, 161, 188

McLoughlin, Barry, 275

McRae, Earl, 62

Mehrabian, Albert, 173, 277

Mendoza, Martha, 86-88

Mohn, Tanya, 131

Moss, Kate, 39, 45

Moulthrop, Dan, 204-205

Nelson, Dean, 178, 272

Nixon, Richard, 210, 264

Norman, Matt, 194

Ojito, Mirta, 73

Paar, Jack, 96

Parker, Dorothy, 170

Pascau, Pierre, 167

Pease, Allan and Barbara, 281

Penacoli, Jerry, 115

Plimpton, George, 127-128

Pocklington, Peter, 205

Pressfield, Steven, 23, 299

Rae, Bob, 51-53, 58

Raft, George, 162

Rather, Dan, 264

Reardon, Kathleen Kelley, 273

Retter, Ken, 99-100

Rice, Jim, 238-239

Riggio, Ronald, 279-280

Robbie, Margot, 119

Rockwell, George Lincoln,
    236-237

Salas, Antonio, 109

Sapir, Avinoam, 146

Sarkozy, Nicolas, 67-68

Sawyer, Diane, 208

Scanlan, Chip, 167

Scruggs, Kathy, 34-35

Seinfeld, Jerry, 77

Sheikh, Knvul, 274

Shields, Brooke, 43

Siegel, Robert, 192

Silverstone, Alicia, 118

Sinatra, Frank, 91-92, 162

Slater, Christian, 133-134

Smyth, Jim (Det. Sgt.), 175

Snyder, Tom, 290-291

Stahl, Lesley, 67-68

Stanfield, Robert, 152-153

Steinem, Gloria, 109

Stern, Howard, 118

Stoynoff, Natasha, 132-133

Susman, Gary, 202

Talese, Guy, 72

Talley, André Leon, 227

Thatcher, Margaret,
    152, 241-242

Theroux, Louis, 164, 169

Thomas, Helen, 141

Thompson, Hunter S., 274

Thornton, Billy Bob, 232-234

Travolta, John, 203-204

Troyer, Warner, 96, 214

Trudeau, Pierre Elliot, 153

Trump, Donald, 22-23, 49, 86, 132

Turner, Graham, 165

Vartanian, Talin, 57, 297

Vidal, Gore, 97

Wallace, Mike, 38-39, 107

Walters, Barbara, 101, 208

Watson, Emma, 103, 116

Williams, Russell, 174

Winfrey, Oprah, 46, 116, 170, 284

Wise, Hymie, 165

Wolfe, Tom, 274

Woods, Tiger, 89, 262

Wright, Jim, 74

Yzerman, Steve, 153-154

ABOUT THE AUTHOR

Paul McLaughlin is a leading interviewing expert and the author of *Asking Questions: The Art of the Media Interview* (1986). A former interviewing trainer for CBC Radio and TV, he has had a long career as a freelance journalist for both broadcast and print. He has also taught journalism at Algonquin College and Carleton University in Ottawa, and Ryerson University and (currently) York University, in Toronto.

www.paulmclaughlin.ca.